Pathways to Leadership

James Lawrence Powell

Pathways to Leadership

How to Achieve
and Sustain Success

Jossey-Bass Publishers
San Francisco

Substantial discounts on bulk quantities of Jossey-Bass books are available to corporations, professional associations, and other organizations. For details and discount information, contact the special sales department at Jossey-Bass Inc., Publishers. (415) 433–1740; Fax (800) 605–2665.

For sales outside the United States, please contact your local Paramount Publishing International Office.

 Manufactured in the United States of America on Lyons Falls Pathfinder Tradebook. This paper is acid-free and 100 percent totally chlorine-free.

Credits are on page 253.

Library of Congress Cataloging-in-Publication Data

Powell, James Lawrence, date.
  Pathways to leadership : how to achieve and sustain success /
James Lawrence Powell.
    p.   cm. — (The Jossey-Bass nonprofit sector series)
  Includes bibliographical references and index.
  ISBN 0-7879-0094-X
    1. Nonprofit organizations—Management.   2. Chief executive
officers.   3. Leadership.   4. Success in business.   I. Title.
II. Series.
  HD62.6.P69   1995
  658.4′092—dc20 .   94-43956
                                                              CIP

HB Printing   10 9 8 7 6 5 4 3 2 1   FIRST EDITION

The Jossey-Bass
Nonprofit Sector Series

• •

Contents

Preface

Nonprofit organizations include the most respected institutions in American society: universities and colleges, hospitals, churches, foundations, museums, libraries, professional associations, arts and community organizations, welfare and social service agencies, environmental groups, and many others. In quantitative and economic terms, the sector is enormous: more than one million nonprofit organizations exist in the United States and thousands are added each year. Revenues exceed $500 billion (twice as much as the construction industry) and seven million people are employed (Gaul and Borowski, 1993). When the number of volunteers is included, the total reaches more than eighty million people—one out of every two adults. The nonprofit sector is the nation's largest employer (Drucker, 1989, p. 88).

The sector is even more important qualitatively. Without the cultural, educational, and spiritual enrichment that these institutions furnish, the quality of life in America would be unimaginably diminished. Former Health, Education and Welfare Secretary John Gardner wrote, "Virtually every significant social idea in this country has been nurtured in the nonprofit sector" (O'Connell, 1993, p. 5). Clearly, the quality of leadership in the nonprofit sector is an essential national interest.

The Nonprofit Sector and Its Leadership

Each nonprofit organization, no matter how small, has a leader, variously called president, chief executive officer, executive director, or director. (In this book I will refer to them all by the single title of chief executive.) A few have already been the chief executive of another organization, but most are in the position for the first time. Knowing the importance of the nonprofit sector and of their organization, they are prepared to do their best. Once in the job, however, they find themselves with a host of new duties for which their previous positions did not fully prepare them. Suddenly they must deal directly with trustees, give speeches, entertain, hire and fire, and manage a much more complex schedule. At times, the entire weight of the organization seems to rest on their shoulders.

If more nonprofit chief executives had been educated in how to manage organizations, they would find the task easier. Although some have earned an M.B.A. degree, only a few have specialized in nonprofit management or had the opportunity to take even a single course in the subject; until recently, such courses, much less degree programs, have not existed. Fortunately, several major universities and business schools have added course work in nonprofit management (Young, 1990) and several have programs in arts management. Many nonprofit professional organizations conduct workshops and similar professional development activities, including programs for the new chief executive. Universities and business schools operate institutes in educational leadership, some of which focus on nonprofit management.

The new chief executive will benefit greatly from some of the writings on leadership and on the nonprofit sector. John Gardner's *On Leadership* (1990) is an excellent general survey on which it would be hard to improve. James Fisher's *Power of the Presidency* (1984) describes how the academic president can be maximally effective. Fisher again, in *The Board and the President* (1991), tells both parties how they should interact and support each other ideally. Brian

O'Connell's *The Board Member's Book* (1993) gives sound advice to nonprofit directors. Cohen and March, in their classic, *Leadership and Ambiguity* (1986), dissect the modern university presidency. In *Managing the Non-profit Organization: Principles and Practices*, Peter Drucker (1990) describes the management techniques of selected nonprofit leaders. Several other good books could also be named.

What appears to be lacking is a guide to the day-to-day *practice* of leading a nonprofit organization, starting with the question of whether one should aspire to such a position in the first place. If the answer is yes, how do you maximize your chances of getting an offer? Once in the position, what should you do next? What are the most important factors that will determine your survival and success? What is the ideal relationship with the trustees who hire and fire nonprofit chief executives? How do you know when your effectiveness has declined and it is time to go?

This book, written by an experienced nonprofit chief executive, attempts to provide frank, practical advice. Its premise is that, although the job is complex, broad similarities from one nonprofit organization to the next allow the chief executive, especially the new one, to benefit from the experience of others. The major duties of the position, considered one by one, can be successfully accomplished by following commonsense guidelines.

I think of this book as a survivor's manual that shows how the nonprofit chief executive can persist in the job long enough to induce significant change. This concern with longevity in the position comes because the expectations of chief executives rise as their average tenure falls. Academic presidents last for an average of six years; directors of nursing, three; urban school superintendents, less than two. For every nonprofit chief executive who serves for ten to fifteen years, others fail to last a year. Few leaders have so little job security, such leaky parachutes—if indeed they have one at all—and such complex responsibilities. Thus, the first rule for the leader must be, while not compromising important principles, to endure in the position long enough to make a difference.

Perspective of the Book

Anything worth reading must be written from some point of view; mine is more personal and applied than that found in most books on leadership. It would be difficult for anyone to write a book that is practical and experience-based, as this one is, and that covers equally well the entire nonprofit sector, for few if any nonprofit leaders have served at institutions from the smallest through the medium sized to the largest. If any have, as far as I am aware they have not written about their experience. Of necessity, this book reflects my own background at institutions of two hundred to four hundred employees. Some nonprofits are much larger, but many are smaller and some are much smaller. For the following reasons, I believe that the lessons drawn in this book will apply to the broad range of non-profit institutions, from the smallest to the largest. First, my advice is directed to the chief executive, rather than to the institution per se. Many of the duties of the executive are similar across the range. Regardless of the size of the organization, the chief executive interacts on a daily basis with about the same number of people—the "direct reports"—who generally number from three to eight. Second, career paths typically lead from smaller institutions to larger ones; many administrators are on a trajectory that will lead them to service at a bigger organization. Third, the reader can scale down from the larger to the smaller, selecting and adapting what is most pertinent; going the other direction would be more difficult. Fourth, I include many case examples drawn from smaller nonprofits.

Audience

It is my hope that this book will prove useful to several different audiences. The largest group comprises those working in the non-profit sector at various career stages. Newly arrived chief executives are apt to find gaps in their training and experience and little else in the way of assistance. Other nonprofit administrators have reached the point where they have, or soon might have, an offer to become a nonprofit chief executive. Not all who have the opportunity should take it; some would be better off, personally and professionally, by remaining a level or two below the stratum of chief executive. This book provides a framework to assist them in making an informed decision. Then there are those in the middle ranks of administration who may aspire someday to become a chief executive but for whom the decision is years in the future. They may wish to learn more about what the job entails and to improve their own performance by emulating the techniques of successful chief executives. Even those who have no aspiration to be a chief executive may develop such an ambition later; meanwhile, they must deal with a chief executive daily. This book shows how such a person thinks about the job and its priorities. Last are those nonprofit chief executives with a few years of service who are open to benefiting from the experiences of one of their own. Trustees of nonprofits who hire, work with, and dismiss chief executives would benefit from a better appreciation of the chief executive's perspective. Finally, the book will be useful to members of the academic community who have an interest in the practical, as opposed to the theoretical, aspects of nonprofit leadership.

Overview of the Contents

The first step for one who aspires to become a nonprofit chief executive is to perform a rigorous assessment of the reasons for wanting the position—distinguishing those that will lead to success from those that will bring failure and a short tenure. The next is to enter and emerge successfully from the search process—to land the job. These two subjects are covered in Chapter One, which describes the details of nonprofit searches from the perspective of the candidate, who is usually at the mercy of the searching institution. What is it like to go through the different stages of a chief executive search? How do you maximize your chances of getting an offer? How should you conduct yourself so as to exit the process, if not with the job, at least with your dignity and reputation intact?

The premise of this book is that the most effective leader is the one who induces the most beneficial change that the organization can handle successfully. A great deal is now known about leadership: its relation to the evolution of organizations, the most effective role of the leader, the attributes of forceful leaders, the sources of leadership authority. Anyone who aspires to be a nonprofit leader ought to be familiar with the major findings of this scholarship and to consider how best to apply it. This is the subject and purpose of Chapter Two. Though most of what it takes to become an effective leader can be learned, certain aspects of leadership make many people uncomfortable, perhaps more than they are willing to be. As Truman said, "If you can't stand the heat, stay out of the kitchen." The chief executive is in the kitchen, and unlike a family kitchen, it is often a lonely place. Many will not want to make the sacrifice even though they have all the other attributes necessary for leadership. All aspiring leaders, however, should be aware of the findings of research on leadership; otherwise they are flying blind.

The first few weeks and months are critical in any new position. The relationships established and the patterns set often determine how effective the entire tenure will be; some nonprofit executives are never able to recover from early mistakes. Chapter Three discusses how this transition period, or honeymoon, can be used to set the stage for change and for effective leadership and how one can climb the learning curve as the advantages of the honeymoon period wane (Gilmore, 1988). It also shows why the new chief executive should start a program of stress management immediately and how to go about it.

Most who become chief executives have demonstrated ability as administrators. The position of chief executive is different, however: not only is it the most complicated and demanding in the organization but the ability to handle administrative tasks is far from sufficient for success. Now those tasks have to be managed even more efficiently so that the leader has time for thinking and planning. For the first time in your career, you can administer impeccably and fail. Administrative ability is thus a necessary but not a sufficient criterion for success. Chapter Four covers several crucial administrative areas: time management, making meetings productive, the art of delegation, and control and use of information technology.

Evaluating your senior staff associates and sometimes discharging them are essential tasks. Chapter Five describes how to go about them humanely and fairly. Once vacancies for senior positions have arisen by whatever means, how well they are filled will be key in determining the chief executive's success. This chapter goes on to describe how to hire the best person available and to do it in such a way that the appointee gets off to the most promising start.

Nonprofits must balance their budgets. Gaining and maintaining financial stability is a requirement for leadership today. The chief executive's skills, ideas, character, personal relations—all will matter little if the organization runs a deficit for more than a few years. Chapter Six outlines the steps that the chief executive can take to ensure sound financial management and to use the institutional budget as the principal vehicle for change.

To plan is to accept that change is inevitable—planning maps the route by which it will be accomplished. As the world moves at an ever-faster pace, planning becomes increasingly crucial. The sophistication of funders, trustees, and others has reached the point at which an institution that does not have a plan is downgraded. One of the first questions asked today is, "May I see your strategic plan?" Another is apt to be, "Have you used Total Quality Management?" Although it may have been overly touted (and certainly it has been misunderstood by those who have yet to try it), TQM does have something to offer nonprofit organizations. The chief executive must know how to oversee the planning process and how to use the best aspects of TQM. These are covered in Chapter Seven.

Nonprofits exist to fulfill a mission. Unlike a company, whose financial results establish whether it is performing satisfactorily, a nonprofit cannot gauge its effectiveness from its bottom line. This has meant that few nonprofits have found a way to determine how well they are achieving their mission. Most have assumed that good intentions suffice; if they ever did, they do no longer. Increasingly, government and private funders want to know what works and how you know. It is incumbent on nonprofits to the extent possible (which is further than most will imagine) to evaluate their programs and activities. Chapter Eight shows how to evaluate the organization, its administrative operations, and the projects that it conducts.

Chapter Nine reviews the important subject of communication, external and internal. To the external community, the chief executive is the principal and usually the only institutional communicator. Through speeches, the executive has a golden opportunity to enlist those outside the organization in the cause. Most new chief executives, however, have had little opportunity to practice public speaking and find it daunting. They should not, for although the great orators may be born rather than made, anyone with enough skill and intelligence to be a chief executive in the first place can learn to deliver an effective speech. Inside the organization, too little attention is usually paid to communication—often it is left to chance or when the mood happens to strike. People must be persuaded to try change, however, and persuasion requires communication. The vision that the change represents, and its advantages to staff and to the institution, must be clearly communicated. Once an organization begins to implement a strategic plan, staff need a continual supply of information.

Rare is the nonprofit that does not depend to some degree on gifts and grants. To balance the budget therefore requires raising money and the chief executive is the primary fundraiser. In their previous positions, many new chief executives have never had to ask for gifts; now they have no choice. As explained in Chapter Ten, this task is not as difficult as many suppose.

Nor have most nonprofit chief executives interacted directly with trustees, who now make up the executive's key constituency.

The principal responsibility of the board is to hire and sometimes to fire the chief executive. It is critical that the chief executive understand that it is the board for whom the executive works. You forget this elemental fact of executive survival at your peril. The most important relationship is with the chair of the board. Chapter Eleven shows how to interact with this important group so as to enlist them in your program of change.

In any leadership position, a point is eventually reached at which the leader and others know that most of the change that could be induced by that particular executive at that particular institution has been achieved. Chapter Twelve describes how to assess when that time has come and what to do about it. The process through which the position of chief executive is vacated is the undiscussed half of leadership succession; it represents a dire personal difficulty for many nonprofit leaders and on a larger scale is a major national problem that ought to find a national solution.

Conclusion

The cases cited as examples in this book are generally drawn from instances known to me personally. I have altered institutional and individual descriptors so that identities can remain confidential.

When I began this book, I had assumed that my personal experience with the subjects of Chapters One and Three—successfully negotiating one's way through a chief executive search and starting up in a new position—was well behind me. It turned out, however, that during the latter part of the period in which the book was being written, I was contacted by a search consultant and was recruited from my position as president of the Franklin Institute to the equivalent position at the Los Angeles County Museum of Natural History. Thus, I had occasion to test and modify my advice in light of my contemporary experience.

Some in the for-profit sector have deprecated nonprofit leadership as unprofessional and unbusinesslike. Those who do should take a hard look at the record of leadership of the Fortune 500 over the last decade. I believe that nonprofit leadership is more difficult than leadership of comparably-sized for-profit businesses and that to do it well takes more skill. Why? Because nonprofits are more resistant to change than companies; their chief executives have less authority; success is ill-defined and harder to measure; many nonprofits are "organized anarchies." To lead and manage institutions under such difficult conditions requires exceptional skill. Certainly no leadership position allows one to associate with finer people or more vital causes. It is my hope that this book will help the courageous individuals who agree to lead these indispensable organizations to better understand their role, to perform more effectively, and to gain more satisfaction from it.

Acknowledgments

I owe a debt, as do all academic leaders, to the inspirational writings of James Fisher. Those outside the academic sector should become familiar with his works. Brian O'Connell, recently retired as president of the INDEPENDENT SECTOR, encouraged me to write a practical book about nonprofit leadership. My longtime colleagues and superb leaders David Ellis, former president of Lafayette College and director of the Boston Museum of Science, and Charles Glassick, former president of Gettysburg College and president of the Woodruff Center in Atlanta, read the manuscript and made many helpful suggestions. Katherine Coate, director of the Greater Philadelphia Cultural Alliance; Karen Simmons, director of the La Salle University Nonprofit Management Development Center; and Tom Curtis of the Big Brother/Big Sister headquarters in Philadelphia all reviewed an early draft and made many useful comments. My sister, Beth Powell, herself an author, used several days of precious vacation time to read the manuscript. Karen Miselis Goldstein, Ben Goldstein, James Hess, and Dan Updegrove each reviewed chapters. My wife, Joan Hartmann, read the book several

times in its various phases. Our daughter, Joanna, deferred her own
desire to use the family Macintosh on numerous occasions. Barrie
Van Dyck was my expert agent. To all I express my gratitude.

Los Angeles, California   James Lawrence Powell
February 1995

To my mother, Lizena Davis Powell

The Author

· ·

James Lawrence Powell is president and director of the Los Angeles County Museum of Natural History. He received his A.B. degree (1958) in geology from Berea College, Kentucky, and his Ph.D. degree (1962) in geochemistry from the Massachusetts Institute of Technology. He also received two D.Sc. degrees, one (1983) from Oberlin College and the other (1992) from Beaver College, and an Lh.D. degree (1986) from Tohoku Gakuin in Sendai, Japan.

Powell began his career as assistant professor of geology at Oberlin College, where he held a series of posts including acting president. He served as president of Franklin and Marshall College and Reed College and as president and chief executive officer of the Franklin Institute. He has published articles on geology in *Science*, *Nature*, *Journal of Petrology*, *Geochimica et Cosmochimica Acta*, and elsewhere; has written on educational administration; and is co-author of *Strontium Isotope Geology*, published by Springer-Verlag (1972, with G. Faure).

Powell has served as a director of the Association of American Colleges, EDUCOM, the Institute for European Studies, and several other organizations. He was appointed to the National Science Board by President Reagan, was reappointed by President Bush, and has served since 1986.

Pathways to Leadership

Leaders are agents of change.

—Bernard M. Bass,
Bass & Stodgill's Handbook of Leadership

Part I

. . . .

Becoming a Nonprofit CEO

If you are considering a position as a nonprofit chief executive, you should first look inward and ask yourself some important questions: What do you do well? How do you prefer to spend your time? If you did not need to work, what would you choose to do?

Some of the aspects of being a successful leader, such as maintaining a degree of social distance, or coping with a greatly increased level of stress, may call for greater personal sacrifice than you are willing to make. It is best to think the matter through in advance. As the saying goes, be careful what you wish for; you may get it. Whether to accept an offer to become a chief executive is one of the most important decisions in a lifetime and should be approached accordingly.

Once the requisite self-analysis has been done, the task of the aspiring nonprofit chief executive is to get elected—to obtain an offer. The process by which nonprofit chief executives are selected is one of the least perfect of human efforts. Yet thousands of executive searches are conducted annually in the nonprofit sector, so the aspiring chief executive can learn a great deal from the experience of others about how to survive a search with dignity—even if the job does not come through.

Searches have an often overlooked additional importance: the way in which they are conducted can strongly influence, and even determine, the success of the appointee. The nonprofit chief executive who gains office through a flawed process, regardless of who is responsible for the flaw, may be hamstrung. For example, it is not uncommon for a board chair to handpick a chief executive who, having merit but lacking widespread support, lasts only a short time, as this vignette illustrates:

> For several years, the chair of the board of an eastern public university knew whom he wanted as the institution's president: a close friend who was at that time president of another university in the state. When the presidency in question became available, the chair saw to it that his favorite was nominated, but to his dismay, although his man survived the first cut, he failed to make the second. Working behind the scenes, however, the chair arranged for his choice to reemerge in the third stage. This process of removal and resurrection continued several times until the man was selected in a closed-door meeting of trustees. He turned out to be an adequate if not great president, but faculty had been so alienated by the flawed process that he was soon forced to resign.

It is safe to say that few chief executives can overcome the consequences of a severely flawed search. On the other hand, when the community views a search as fair and the new appointee as legitimate, almost everyone will want the new chief executive to succeed (of course, their definitions of what constitutes success will vary); some will be prepared to help. Here is what can happen when a search is not legitimate:

> A small service agency needed to replace its outgoing director. The chair of the board, a busy and powerful corporate CEO, met the director of another agency (one with a quite different mission) and thought that she would make an excellent choice. Just as he would have done in his business, he invited the woman in for lunch and offered her the post, which after a few days she accepted. The chair then called the other trustees to tell them that the new director had

been selected. Several expressed surprise, but none formally objected. After a few months, however, it became clear that the new director was not well-suited to the agency and that she was at a disadvantage because she was not given the benefit of the doubt by trustees and staff, most of whom had not heard of her before she arrived. She quickly resigned, her career damaged. The executive committee of the board determined that it would not allow this mistake to be repeated; another quick exit by a chief executive would destroy the agency's image and credibility. A small search committee was formed that included a local search consultant working pro bono. The search was conducted professionally and a fine candidate was hired. Because they had participated, trustees and senior staff were now invested in the new executive's success; she went on to be an outstanding leader.

Those who aspire to become leaders need to learn as much as possible about the nature of leadership and power, a fascinating subject. Though aspects of leadership remain mysterious, in recent years a great deal has been learned that the new chief executive can put to good use. With the possible exception of the truly great leaders of history, it is clear that leaders are made, not born. The attributes that contribute to leadership can be understood, developed, and employed, and each nonprofit executive should endeavor to do so.

The first few months in a new leadership position, which are ideally a honeymoon period, are critical. The relationships, work patterns, and agenda that are established are apt to remain for the rest of the leader's tenure. One key to a successful honeymoon is to avoid major mistakes (some minor ones are unavoidable). The longer major errors can be postponed, the longer and more effective will be the honeymoon. Use this time carefully to establish your credibility and to demonstrate that you understand the necessary balance between tradition and renewal. Lay the foundation for change brick by brick.

The job of chief executive is almost without exception the most stressful that anyone new to such a position has ever had. Chief executives who are unwilling to recognize this fact and to do something about it are asking for trouble. Stress management is not a sign of weakness. In fact, it is just the opposite: managing stress shows maturity and professionalism and is as important, perhaps more important, to you and your family than anything else you do. Begin your program of stress management during the honeymoon.

1

Navigating the Executive Search Process

We seek him here, we seek him there,
Those Frenchies seek him everywhere.
Is he in heaven? Is he in hell?
That demmed, elusive Pimpernel?
            Baroness Orczy, The Scarlet Pimpernel

The first step in the process of becoming a nonprofit leader is to rigorously assess your strengths and abilities and honestly examine your reasons for aspiring to such a position. Unless those reasons are sound, success will prove elusive. The second step is to emerge from the executive search process with the job you sought or, failing that, to learn something useful while retaining your self-respect. Large institutions such as a substantial museum, a university, or the headquarters of a national service agency follow the full set of job-search procedures described in this chapter. Many smaller organizations go to less elaborate lengths, conducting, for example, local rather than national searches. The essential stages are similar regardless of size, however: candidates are nominated or apply and are screened, a few are invited for one or more interviews, references are checked, a selection is made, a negotiation takes place, an offer is formally accepted.

Gauging Your Potential

Not everyone has the qualities or the drive to be a successful chief executive. An individual can be right for a certain organization but not for others. Before approaching such a position, the prospective chief executive should give careful thought to the degree of fit and, equally important, to whether the job would be enjoyable. Without such an analysis, the chief executive may either fail and have to bail out quickly, sustaining career damage, or struggle on in the post, performing poorly and unhappily. In the first case, the institution will need to search again soon; in the second, it will have to endure a long and ineffective tenure. Better to spend some time communing with yourself and with trusted friends, carefully assessing your ability and the fit.

Criteria for Success

To be successful, both the chief executive and the organization must meet certain criteria such as those described in the following paragraphs.

You as prospective chief executive must be able to support the institution's mission sincerely and enthusiastically; the executive will be called upon to do so repeatedly, and no one likes a hypocrite. Ideally, the mission will coincide with your deeply held beliefs, allowing you to put the institution's cause above your own self-interest. If not, beware. For example, if your main interest is in museum education, you ought not to become the director of a museum that focuses largely on its collections. If you are fundamentally unsympathetic with the beneficiaries of the work of a social service agency, you cannot lead that agency successfully. If you doubt the merit of single-sex education, you ought not to become president of a women's college. Only those whose main motivation is to help a nonprofit organization provide the kind of service for which it was chartered are apt to remain long in the job and to make a lasting difference.

The organization must appear to have a proper balance between authority and responsibility: it can be led and, though it may not be easy, will accept well-planned change. In order to judge, talk with knowledgeable people, including some who have left the institution. In the end, though, you may simply have to make an educated guess on this point.

After a good deal of self-analysis, you must not only believe yourself to be capable of being a chief executive, you must be ready to work hard at it and to put up with increased stress. Talk with a few chief executives and ask what they like and dislike about their jobs.

The compensation and perquisites must be reasonable. Speak confidentially with a current chief executive, an association officer, or a search consultant about what would constitute a fair range of compensation.

You must be willing to put up with conflict and to relish making decisions even knowing that some people, or many, will be displeased with you. The saying is that each time a chief executive makes a decision, 5 percent of the constituents are angry, but with each decision it is a different 5 percent. By the time twenty decisions have been made, everyone is angry at the chief executive over something!

If you have a family or significant other, the potential move must be discussed thoroughly with them and they must be supportive. Many a marriage has collapsed after it was discovered too late that a spouse was unwilling to move to the new location. (The opposite problem arises when the spouse and family truly want to move but the offer does not come. Sometimes the family has more trouble handling this disappointment than does the candidate.) Many chief executive positions place specific demands on the spouse and on family relations; if so, these demands need to be discussed in advance. Executives who work in the arts could be out each night of the week if they chose; those who work in human services can become overwhelmed by the seeming intractability of the problems their agency addresses.

Finally, you ought to feel that the position is likely to bring you enjoyment and satisfaction. You cannot be an effective leader and hide your dislike of the job for very long; you will fail professionally and personally. Many chief executives have tried to go on in a job they disliked and have found themselves trapped and depressed. For that reason, I respect those who, having taken on the position of chief executive, recognize their mistake and exit quickly.

Criteria for Failure

Some people, though talented, are simply not cut out to be chief executives; the personal costs are too high. Others, who have the ability and are willing to accept the cost, may find that the problems of some organizations are so difficult that "God on a good day" could not solve them (as the late Father Tim Healy is said to have described the job of a university president). Further, even if you have the inherent ability to be a chief executive and the problems of the institution are manageable, success may be elusive unless the real motivation for taking the job is sound. Among the worst reasons for pursuing such a position are to bolster the ego, to make more money, and to gain power. Each of these is worth examining briefly.

Of course, ego drives much of human behavior and no one can succeed as a leader without a healthy dose of it. The successful chief executive takes action in part for the good of the organization and in part because success will bring acclaim and reward. All this is understandable, but balance is important. Actions taken more out of self-interest than on behalf of the institution will result in an early departure by the chief executive and a weakened institution.

Salary is a serious consideration in any job, for both personal and familial reasons. An increase in salary is a reasonable, in some cases a necessary, expectation for any new position, but it is far from sufficient grounds for taking on the responsibilities of chief executive. After all, salary is usually proportionate to difficulty: as salary increases, so will responsibility and the price paid in stress and time constraints. Nonprofit chief executives certainly earn their salaries, which in any case are low in comparison with similar jobs in the for-profit sector.

Power is an inevitable aspect of leadership, as we will explore in the next chapter. It derives in part from the ability of the leader to coerce and to reward certain desired behaviors. Yet power contains the seeds of its own destruction, as expressed by Lord Acton in his famous aphorism, "Power tends to corrupt; absolute power corrupts absolutely" (1887). The nonprofit executive who fails to heed this advice and who pursues power for its own sake will fail and do great damage in the process.

The Search

After you have undertaken a careful analysis and concluded that you may indeed have the combination of ability and motivation to be a successful chief executive, how do you find out whether anyone else would agree? One strategy is to wait until you happen to be nominated; another is to apply directly. In the smaller institutions, there is no reason not to apply. In the larger ones, a direct application can lower your chances of being considered seriously. In a reverse twist on Groucho Marx's disinclination to join any club with standards so low that he could be admitted, the principle seems to be that no large organization would want to be led by someone interested enough to apply for the job. Of course, some of the best candidates are less apt to apply directly for a position because they already have good jobs; they need to be sought out and persuaded to toss their hat in the ring. On the other hand, such candidates in the end often prefer to stay where they are, leaving many nonprofit chief executive positions for those who applied. The irony is that in any search, a significant number of those who have been nominated have asked a colleague to put their name forward: they have applied, but the search committee has no way of knowing it. Thus, it makes little sense to give a lower ranking to someone merely because that person applied openly.

From the candidate's perspective, nothing is wrong with asking a colleague for a nomination; it happens many times in every search. It results in the important psychological shift of being invited to be a candidate rather than having to ask for permission. If you do ask a colleague for a letter of nomination, request that it be of the same length and content as a letter of recommendation; that will make a better impression on the search committee.

If you apply directly, prepare your letter carefully. Surprisingly, many fail to grasp the importance of this first contact and fire off a short letter with errors, which suggests to the reviewers that the candidate is not willing or able to put much thought into the position and may be unable to write a decent letter. The letter should go through several revisions and be error-free.

The First Search

In your first search, you will be relatively inexperienced. Enter primarily to gain seasoning; put your best foot forward but be prepared to lose gracefully. This search will not be your last. On the other hand, do not become a serious candidate for any position that you would be likely to turn down in the end. Too many go through a lengthy search process only to decline for a reason that should have been apparent from the outset: the sudden discovery that the family does not wish to move; that the city is not attractive; that no opportunities exist for the spouse; that the salary is after all too low. This wastes time and money and is basically unprofessional. The following case is unfortunately not as rare as it should be:

> A social service agency conducted a national search for a vice pres-
> ident and chose a candidate on the opposite coast, who showed
> interest and was flown in twice for interviews. The agency extended
> a generous offer but received no reply from the candidate for several
> days. Finally, a telephone call elicited the response that the candidate
> had to decline the offer because the spouse did not want to move to
> the new location. Discreet inquiries revealed that the candidate had

used the offer as the basis for a promotion at the home institution, which raised the question of whether the candidate had ever seriously considered the move. Such unprofessional behavior is never forgotten.

In view of the many thousands of nonprofit searches being conducted each year by some of the more intelligent and well-credentialed members of our society, one would think that the search process itself would by now be as close to perfection as any human activity. Alas, in this instance at least, practice has not made perfect. Most search committees start from scratch, repeating the mistakes of their predecessors while inventing new ones. It is not hard to understand why. First, many organizations have an exalted view of the desirability of the position of chief executive at their institution. Staff and even trustees, who should know better, imagine that thousands would give their eyeteeth to lead the organization and regard the post as so uniquely desirable that the conduct of the search matters little. Second, nonprofit searches are often conducted entirely by busy volunteers who do not give enough time and attention to the task. (In that case, the skill and dedication of the chair of the search committee is critical.) Third, those who conduct one search are unlikely to conduct the next, so experience fails to carry over. If one search was successful, the next search will be at least several years later, and the participants are apt to have moved on. If the first search was not successful and the next search begins soon thereafter, those who were responsible are apt to be tarred with the same brush as the failed executive. Hubris, lack of attention, and inexperience are thus the rule, and the search process lurches along, doing a disservice to individuals and institutions.

Recently, the increasing use of professional search consultants has brought about a dramatic improvement. These experts know how searches should be conducted and they are aware that no institution today is irresistible to the prospective candidate. As explained further in Chapter Five, important searches should use consultants. Still, an organization might ignore the consultant's advice or not use a consultant at all. Expect the worst and you will not be disappointed.

The Early Stages

If you have been nominated, the first contact from the institution is apt to be a letter or telephone call inquiring whether you wish to become a candidate. If the nomination was unsolicited, give careful consideration to the criteria outlined above. If you decide to accept, carefully craft your letter. At this early stage, the strategy of the search committee will be to divide applications and nominations into A, B, and C groups. Your goal is to be well within the A's. Your willingness to become a candidate should be based on knowledge of the institution and its mission and accomplishments, as well as on an assessment of the fit with your interests and abilities. When contacted, you may need to learn more about the institution in order to make this judgment and to prepare your response. Do not provide the search committee with any unsolicited material— including letters of recommendation, which are largely a waste of time at any stage—and at this stage, do not ask them for anything. Follow their procedures and timetable.

The Middle Stages

If the search committee remains interested, you will continue to hear from them. (If it does not, and if the search is not being run professionally, you may never hear anything. More than one candidate has learned that another was chosen by reading about it in the newspaper.) Carefully study the material sent. One of the items is apt to be the job description, which, unless the institution has done a professional audit, describes a candidate who can walk on water. Read it anyway; someone there may believe it. If there is a search consultant, ask for a description of the search process, which might differ in some important way from the generic search described here. The search committee will narrow its list from the total pool of applicants and nominees down to a more manageable number drawn from its A list. At this stage, you may be asked for names of people who can serve as references. Choose people in whose confidentiality you have complete faith (see the following section for more advice on this subject); do not name your current boss at this point. Before representatives of the search make any calls, contact your references to explain why you are in the search and where it stands.

The committee may also ask you for a longer written statement describing your interest; obviously such a statement is subject to the same rules as was your initial letter. You may be asked for samples of your writings and other evidence of your skills and accomplishments.

Confidentiality

One critical decision is when to tell your current supervisor that you are a candidate for a position elsewhere. The cardinal rule of reporting is never surprise your boss. On the other hand, you need to protect your own interests, for no one else is apt to do so. Unless you are certain that your candidacy will become public, you need not inform your boss when you first enter a search. When you reach the point of going to the institution for interviews, however, or when your candidacy may become known for some reason, the time has come. Even if the search is supposedly confidential, there is a good chance that persons outside the search committee will learn of your visit. It is wise to assume that your boss will discover your candidacy and be surprised not to have heard of it from you. By the time of an on-site interview, you are one of a handful of finalists and the odds that you might leave have increased. Your boss will need to begin to think about how to replace you in case it becomes necessary. Be careful, however, not to burn any bridges that you may need to recross.

Most of the time, if approached properly, your present supervisor will understand that you and other subordinates should have opportunities to advance in your careers and be pleased that another institution is confirming the chief executive's good judgment about you. (If your boss does not feel this way, you should be thinking about moving on in any case.) Understand, however, that whenever you tell your boss you are being interviewed for another position, you incur some risk: some will never forgive you for what they perceive as a lack of loyalty. (If you are a sitting chief executive, special advice is given below.)

Confidentiality benefits both individual candidates and the searching institution, as this example illustrates:

> In spite of conducting its search without a consultant, a prestigious art museum had assembled an excellent group of three finalists for its directorship (the next few candidates on the list, however, were viewed as weak). As the finalists prepared to come for public interviews, a newspaper reporter managed to learn their names from a member of the search committee. She then ran an article that identified each of the three and quoted extensively and critically from persons at their home institutions, including trustees who expressed surprise to learn of their chief executive's candidacy, especially from a reporter. Two of the candidates immediately withdrew, claiming to have been engaged only in exploratory discussions and discovered that they much preferred to stay where they were. The third dutifully appeared for interviews but soon received such an attractive counterproposal from her home institution that she declined the museum's subsequent offer. In near desperation, the museum hired its less attractive fourth candidate; two years later, the museum was searching again.

The Chief Executive as Candidate

How do you proceed when you already are a chief executive? Very carefully. After all, nonprofit chief executives are not supposed to think of leaving; they are expected to show unswerving loyalty until the moment that the institution's board decides it no longer needs them. If the institution discovers that its chief executive has willingly entered a search, support will often decline, and in some extreme cases the chief executive will be asked to resign. This case makes the point:

> The board of a Midwestern university had identified the man they wanted as their next president. The process proceeded with confidentiality, until the names of the four finalists were leaked. An enterprising reporter then discovered that earlier in the career of the preferred candidate, he had been criticized for a remark about the jumping prowess of black athletes. Unable to defend himself, he withdrew and returned to his home institution. He had neglected, however, to inform his board of his active involvement in the search, and when they discovered it, they fired him. The notoriety of the search caused the other finalists to withdraw and, because of the timing of the meeting at which the selection was to be announced, the board found itself having to produce and appoint another candidate within two days.

A sitting chief executive can take several steps that will help to protect confidentiality:

Do not enter a search that does not use a consultant. Try for as long as possible to deal only with the consultant.

Do not enter a search in which the committee has not explicitly addressed the question of confidentiality. They should have discussed the special case of the sitting chief executive.

Restrain yourself from initially expressing direct interest in the position. Wait until the search has advanced to the point where serious interest has been expressed in you.

Keep a low profile. Avoid a public appearance at the institution for as long as possible.

Ask for a two-stage process. If the institutional culture requires that any chief executive be openly interviewed at the institution before the appointment, first ask to visit the institution and meet privately with key figures. (In spite of everyone's best efforts, however, your candidacy may become known at this stage.) After this private visit is concluded, if the institution asks you to return for a series of public interviews and meetings, ask the consultant where you rank. (Keep in mind that in any search, the strategy of the search committee is to maximize its options by retaining as many good candidates as possible for as long as possible and that the search representative naturally will put your candidacy in the most optimistic light.) Unless you find that you are first or tied for first or you have already made a decision to leave your current position even without another offer, exit the search. If the institution is not using a consultant and you cannot get an accurate reading of your standing, you must decide how much risk you are willing to take. If you do decide to return for additional interviews, you must now tell your board chair. If you have the right kind of relationship, this conversation should not jeopardize your present position. (But it might.)

In the end, the chief executive must work within, and respect, the culture of the hiring institution. If tradition requires that the candidate compete openly for the position, one who arrives without having done so will be compromised immediately and probably will be headed for an early departure.

The Internal Candidate

The candidate who already has a position at the searching institution is a special case. That person has the advantage of knowing more about the organization than any external candidate could know; but the converse is also true—the candidate from inside is apt to be too well known to be an attractive prospect. An internal candidate who has the authority to be an agent of change will have already made tough decisions and have alienated some at the institution. Therefore, when qualifications are roughly equal, the job is more likely to go to an external candidate. This case shows how a deserving acting chief executive can lose the job:

The director of a mid-sized theater suddenly resigned for personal reasons. The board, needing to act quickly, appointed the associate director, who had been at the theater for twelve years, to be acting director while a search was conducted. She stated her willingness to be a candidate for the position if the board wished her to, which it did. The search took much longer than anyone had expected, forcing the acting director, for the good of the theater, to take strong but legitimate action in several areas. Various of these actions alienated one or another member of the board and senior staff, causing the search process to pass her by in favor of an external candidate who gave a smashing interview but who subsequently proved ineffective. The theater soon embarked on another search, but by that time this conscientious woman was serving as the successful head of a larger theater.

This tipping of the scales toward an outsider is not all bad because in general, institutions will benefit by bringing in someone with new ideas and new questions and individuals will grow and contribute more by moving on. As John Gardner (1990) puts it, "For many institutions faced with the need for renewal . . . only from outside can one be sure of disinterested criticism, astringent appraisal, the rude question [and] judgments untainted by the loyalty and camaraderie of insiders, undistorted by the comfortable assumptions held within the walls" (p. 130). Exceptions exist, of course. The internal candidate should not have high hopes, however; in the end, the post often will and often should go to an outsider. The internal candidate who in spite of these odds is offered the position of chief executive after a careful search can accept with special confidence.

Face-to-Face

The search committee eventually will cull its list down to a smaller number, perhaps six to eight, for face-to-face meetings, most likely off-site, perhaps at an airport hotel. This one- or two-hour interview will probably be with a subset of the search committee. If you have made it this far, give some thought to the kinds of questions you are apt to be asked and practice responses in your head. Resource A lists some generic questions that you may wish to review.

You will undoubtedly be nervous; remind yourself that you are in this search largely for experience. Advancing further would be a pleasant, if unexpected, surprise. You can be confident that you are qualified; otherwise, you would not have gotten this far. Relax and be yourself. Ultimately you cannot be anyone else, and surely it would not only be dishonest but self-defeating to get the job under false pretenses. Be on your best behavior and at your sharpest, surely, but "to thine own self be true."

Soon after you return from this screening interview, the search committee should inform you of its next step. If you are rejected, chalk it up to experience. It will usually prove futile to attempt to learn why you were rejected, although a good search consultant will be able to provide some information. Instead of a rejection, however, you may receive an invitation to come to the institution to meet the full search committee and other key figures.

The On-Site Interview

Read the information about the membership of the search committee, but do not commit it to memory and do not plan to recognize each member by name during your first interview; this smacks of being overprepared and reveals an unseemly degree of interest. Remember that the search committee is looking for someone who is willing to explore the position but who is not desperate to have it.

At larger organizations, be prepared for an exhausting schedule. There, the search process often seems designed to select the winner in a kind of Darwinian struggle for survival of the fittest. You will arrive and depart perhaps thirty-six to forty-eight hours later and will be booked from breakfast to late at night with few if any breaks.

(When it comes your turn to oversee a search, remember how you felt and give candidates time to catch their breath.) To maintain your energy and composure, try to follow these simple good-health guidelines:

- Do not drink during the visit, or at most have a single drink at dinner. You need your wits about you at all times. Your conversational ability and demeanor are being examined constantly, and at meals you may be asked to say a few words, even to give a short, impromptu speech. The committee will be watching you like a hawk, ready for any sign of an inordinate fondness for the grape or poor table manners. You will be keyed up and either exhausted or full of adrenaline; alcohol will not help. Remember Hamlet: "Refrain tonight, and that shall lend a kind of easiness to the next abstinence" (*Hamlet*, 3.4.166).

- Do not smoke in public during the interview. (If you do smoke, stop! Stopping will not only prolong your life, it will aid your career; many people are prejudiced against candidates who smoke.)

- Pace yourself as much as you can. If you are lucky enough to be able to go back to your room, try to take a short nap or at least close your eyes and relax.

- If you get regular exercise, include it in your schedule. An early morning jog is a good way to see the institution and its environs; your regular swim will leave you refreshed and alert.

During the interviews and visits themselves, remember that those with whom you meet are not looking for exact answers. In fact, nothing would seem so dangerous and undesirable as a candidate who could tell a search committee how to solve the problems of the institution without ever having set foot there. More realistically, no candidate would seem so naive as one who thought it possible. Instead, searchers want to discover how you handle questions. Are you a good listener? Do you pause long enough to contemplate both the question and your answer? Are you thoughtful and articulate?

By the time you reach this point in your career, you will have a record. You will be most effective if you point to it, saying, for example, "Of course, I would have to be with your organization for a while to know exactly how to address that problem, but here is how I handled a similar one." On the other hand, if you honestly do not know the answer, do not fake a response. State that you do not know, then explain how you would go about finding out. Remember that the worst interviews are those in which answers must be dragged out of a candidate and the opposite, those in which the interviewers cannot get a word in edgewise. Strike a balance that suits you.

You should not only answer questions but ask some of your own. By doing so, you will acquire some valuable information and demonstrate that you have done your homework. Though these questions will vary with the organization, many are generic. Some could be asked of a search committee; others should be asked of board members only:

1. Were I to join you, how would we know when I had succeeded?

2. What is the financial condition of the organization?

3. What are the most significant problems that you would want me to address?

4. Do the board and the staff agree on this list and its ranking?

5. Why is the current executive leaving and what are his or her plans?

The first question above does not refer to how you would be evaluated for a raise, but rather what the organization would view as a successful executive performance. How this question is answered (if it can be answered at all) and who answers it will be instructive. For example, one candidate asked the search committee this question and was met by a long silence, puzzled looks, and finally by vague platitudes. The candidate took the position, only to have the job turn out to be radically different from the picture presented to him during the search.

Many search decisions, especially the elimination of candidates, are made in the first fifteen minutes of the interview. To satisfy yourself on this point, remember interviews that you have conducted, or think of houses that you have contemplated buying. Just as one can rule out many houses merely by standing on the sidewalk or certainly upon entering them, many candidates are ruled out in the first few minutes of an interview. Few jobs are won in those early minutes, but many are lost. Once a negative impression is established, it is hard to reverse, just as one almost never goes back to revisit a house one rejected upon entry (Gilmore, 1988). Perhaps such quick judgments are unfair, but in love, employment, and house-hunting, they are made constantly. We know what we like. Therefore, be on your toes, especially at the beginning: if you are being interviewed by a committee, start by addressing the questioner but then move your gaze from person to person and make eye contact with each; sit up straight; be yourself, do not pose; answer directly but succinctly. Act like a leader.

At medium-sized and larger institutions, the spouses of candidates are often asked to come along on one of the visits. One can debate the propriety of this in the age of the two-career couple, not to mention the extent to which it is fair to candidates without spouses, but it happens. If you have a spouse, it is not practicable for you to decline to bring him or her along—that may raise even more questions. The institution will wish to observe the kind of person with whom you have chosen to spend your life and to determine how good an ambassador your spouse will be. Although a job is never won by a spouse, it can be lost because of a spouse.

The Exit Interview

Before you leave the interview site, make sure that you have determined the timetable for the remainder of the search. Arrange to speak alone at least for a few minutes with the person to whom you would report as chief executive, probably the chair of the board. Use this opportunity for several purposes:

- *To discuss the range of compensation for the position.* Do not close any doors, however. At this stage, you are apt to be asked to reveal your current compensation (see below).

- *To ask what the main issues are that your prospective boss would wish you to address.* (This subject will be broached again if an offer is extended; see below.)

- *To express your desire for the job.* If you still want the job, this is the time—during a one-on-one conversation with your prospective boss—to make it clear that you do. Any apparent coyness at this late stage will not be appreciated. State honestly but optimistically how you size up the organization and the challenge, but show that you are sincerely attracted to the position.

- *To observe the chemistry, or lack of it, that you have with your boss-to-be.* This is the person with whom you will spend a great deal of time and who will have more influence on your fate than anyone. Observe body language, eye contact, any surreptitious glances at a wristwatch, and so forth.

If this conversation has gone well, the odds that you will get an offer have gone up significantly.

Back at Home

Eventually, although for a while it may seem doubtful, the visit will be over and you will be back at home. The timetable will immediately begin to collapse; searches never end early and seldom end on time. If your first contact after returning is a letter from an official of the search process, the chances are that you have been rejected. Too few organizations are courteous enough to call to tell you the bad news, although given all that you and they have put into your candidacy, they should (and consultants generally will). Do not take a rejection personally or let it sap your self-confidence. Searches are notoriously idiosyncratic and unpredictable. Even if God on a good day were to show up as a candidate, a group of atheists would prefer someone else!

Unless you have a competing offer, never call to find out the status of the search. When the committee has something to tell you, it will. If you happen to have another offer, however, call the appropriate representative of the organization and state that although you remain interested, you have a contending firm offer with a deadline to which you must adhere. This is a sure way to ferret out their degree of interest, but do not bluff.

Ideally, you will receive a call saying that you are the first choice and expressing the hope that terms acceptable to both parties can be found. This call might be from the chair of the search committee or from the search consultant. Having offered you the job, this person is now responsible to the search committee for persuading you to accept. At this moment, you have the most leverage you will ever have with that particular organization, or perhaps in your entire career. The organization does not want to go to its next choice or, heaven forbid, to start the onerous process over. Use this golden opportunity wisely. Seek a compensation package that is fair to you and your family but that is also fair to the organization. You will be respected for driving a hard bargain (the business people on the search committee did so for themselves and have a package well beyond any that you could hope to receive). Everyone will be

better off if you arrive feeling wanted and well-treated. Review the
suggestions in Resource B and note the following ground rules:

Review your current compensation. Sometime in the early stages
of the search process, you should have made a list showing your
salary and each fringe benefit and perquisite of your present position. Place a dollar figure on each. Since several months will go by
between the time of your acceptance and the time of your arrival,
adjust your salary and benefit package up to the level you would
expect to receive in the following year. Unless the offer is higher
than that, you will lose money by accepting. Given the hidden and
incalculable costs of moving, relocating, finding a home, and so
forth, professionals ought to be receive a significant compensation
increase when they change jobs. The intangibles, such as the
perceived quality of life in the new community versus the one that
you know, will remain just that and may make a difficult decision
more so.

Talk to the chair now. If the person with whom you are negotiating is the search consultant, establish whether he or she has the
authority to make a binding agreement. Do not accept the offer
without speaking with the person to whom you will report, who in
all likelihood will be the chair of the board of trustees. If you do not
detect real enthusiasm for your candidacy, beware. Often a search
committee will have its way in the final choice despite the reserva-
tions of the board chair, who defers in a spirit of collegiality that
proves temporary. Once you are on the job, however, the search
committee will disband, never to be heard from again. Most will
continue to support you, but they now exist only as individuals with
varying degrees of influence. Those who preferred other candidates
or who wanted the job themselves may become your first and most
bitter critics. (One chief executive in his second year was confronted by an angry member of the search committee—a lover of
the status quo—who was upset because the chief executive unexpectedly now appeared to "have his own agenda.") But the chair of

the board, the person on whom your career will now largely depend, will remain. Better to determine the true expectations and commitment of the chair now. This following case illustrates the problem:

> The strong-willed chair of the board of a combined art institute and museum had always had his own ideas about the kind of person the institution needed for its next chief executive: a fundraiser. As the search committee—trustees, faculty, students, staff, and alumni—continued to work, the profile of the chief executive that emerged was that of an educator. The chair chose not to voice his objections. A person with an exemplary record in education was selected but in spite of an outstanding performance never found favor with the chair, who retained his preference for a fundraiser. Soon the institution was engaged in another search, using exactly the same process.

Get a written contract and read it carefully. Eventually, perhaps after several exchanges, you will come to terms that are acceptable to you and to the institution. Get the offer in writing, in the form of a term contract, and read it carefully to make sure that it covers every item that you discussed. You may be wise to have an attorney standing by to give it a quick reading. Understand, however, that the organization will be eager to move quickly because it has other candidates waiting in the wings in case you decline. These candidates may be in other searches with their own deadlines, or they may get cold feet if they detect insufficient interest. Therefore, conclude the negotiations within one or two days.

A final piece of advice: after accepting the offer, leave your old organization as soon as possible. It is human nature to overestimate one's own importance. You will be tempted to believe, perhaps feeling slightly guilty about leaving, that you ought to stay for many months, until your successor is named and on board. This is simply wrong. Once you announce that you are leaving (or unfortunately even when word gets out that you have been on the job market), your effectiveness declines: you have become a lame duck (possibly a dead duck) and your colleagues have already begun to think beyond you. In some cases, you may be able to arrange a paid terminal leave. This advice is predicated on the assumption that like any good manager, you have a person reporting to you who could step in competently were you to leave for any reason. If you do not have such a person, find one as soon as you can.

2

Understanding Leadership

*Of a good leader, who talks little, when his work is
done, his aim fulfilled, they will all say, "We did this
ourselves."*

Lao-Tzu, The Way of Life

The search is over and you have either won the job you wanted
or gained valuable experience that will help you in the next
one. Assuming that you landed the job, you are now about to
embark on your new position as the chief executive of an important
nonprofit institution. As you do so, it is time again to consider the
deep reasons for accepting such a position. One is transcendent: to
provide leadership to a cause in which you believe deeply. If you do
not truly aspire to lead or do not feel passionately about the cause,
beware: you are apt to wind up cheating the organization, subvert-
ing the profession of leadership, and failing personally. This chapter summarizes the findings or research on leadership and provides a
framework for understanding how leadership can be studied, understood, and developed. The key is that leaders are not born—they
are made.

Leadership and Change

What is leadership about, at root? In the epigraph that opens this
book, Bernard Bass, perhaps the outstanding authority, states that

leaders are agents of change (1990, p. 19), using *agent* in the sense of the third definition of Webster's *Tenth New Collegiate Dictionary*, "a means or instrument by which a guiding intelligence achieves a result." Leadership is about change: the most effective leaders are able to induce or extract the maximum amount of change that their organization can sustain; less effective leaders accept the diminished role of protector of the status quo. James MacGregor Burns (1978) defined the difference between the leader who accepts the organization as it is and makes little or no effort at improving it—the transactional leader—and the one who, rather than merely accepting existing values, transforms them—the transformational leader. Abraham Lincoln, as shown so well by Garry Wills in his masterful *Lincoln at Gettysburg* (1992), is the archetypal American transformational leader: while renewing the dedication of Americans to their Constitution, Lincoln transformed the very concept of the United States.

Ultimately, without a larger goal than protecting the status quo, people and organizations stultify. Since everything around them—politics, economics, demographics, technology—is changing on a faster scale than ever these days, organizations must respond or find themselves superseded by those that are more adaptable. However, organizations cannot change unless people change. Without new knowledge, new challenges, new skills, people grow less productive and less happy; personal and professional lives become tiresome and unrewarding. An organization that does not provide sufficient opportunity for growth will cause its employees to lose heart. The best will move to more flexible organizations; those without that option will stay.

Surely, then, change will be welcomed, even embraced. Alas, change is by definition inconvenient: one must go to the trouble of discarding the old, comfortable ways of doing things and attempt to learn new ways. At best, this will take time. At worst, people fear that they may spend the time but prove unable to master the new techniques, or having mastered them, will discover they are no better than the old. For these and other reasons, it appears to be in the immediate interest of individuals to resist change, and many do. In every organization, there are some who believe that the status quo is not just one option, it is the only option. Ogden Nash (1975) captured their plaintive motto: "Progress might have been all right once, but it has gone on for far too long" (p. 98).

The nonprofit chief executive cannot overcome this attitude by decree; rather, various constituencies must be persuaded. Working within the governance system of the organization, the effective leader makes such a compelling case for a proposed change that individuals see how both they and the organization will benefit. When persuasion is successful and positive, change results, and the wise leader, following the advice of Lao-Tzu, will let followers receive the credit.

The leader should not always push the edge of the envelope of change; institutions have the capacity for only so much adjustment at a time. The leader's task is to sort out from all the possible changes those that will allow the organization to progress most productively in fulfilling its mission. Just as one geological stratum cannot be deposited until the previous one has been laid down, between periods of building there must be time for consolidation. It is important to know what can be changed and when, but especially what ought *not* to be changed. A good leader is conscious of tradition and does not espouse any and all possible changes—only those that enable the institution to better achieve its mission. Further, to spend valuable time and energy on what should not or cannot be changed carries a heavy cost.

Sources of Leadership

Many scholars have defined leadership: Bass (1990) reviews the literature thoroughly; Fisher (1991, p. 12) defines leadership in terms of differential power as "the ability of A to get B to do something that B might otherwise not have done"; Burns (1978, p. 18) states,

"Leadership over other human beings is exercised when persons with certain motives and purposes mobilize, in competition or conflict with others, institutional, political, psychological and other resources so as to arouse, engage and satisfy the motives of followers;" and Gardner (1990, p. 1) says that "Leadership is the process of persuasion or example by which an individual (or leadership team) induces a group to pursue objectives held by the leader or shared by the leader and his or her followers."

Max Weber (1947) wrote that leadership derives from three sources: tradition, legality, or charisma. French and Raven (1959), in a taxonomy that has been widely discussed and used, classified the bases of power into five interrelated categories: coercive, reward, legitimate, expert, and referent (for which I will temporarily use Weber's word, *charismatic*). Galbraith (1983) wrote that the sources of power are condign, compensatory, and conditional, the latter of which subsumes legitimate, expert, and charismatic power. Bell (1975) shows how power, influence, and authority, although overlapping, provide a useful framework for understanding interactions between leaders and followers. This book will show how the five sources identified by French and Raven can be classified under Bell's tripartite structure.

Power

Power is reflected by the statement "If you do X, I will do Y," where Y may be negative, as in the use of *coercion*, or positive, as in the use of *reward* (Bell, 1975). Coercion, the threat or actuality of punishment, eventually fails and should be used most sparingly. On the other hand, the executive who fails to use coercion under any circumstances—for example, by refusing to discipline a staff member who deserves it—or who fails even to acknowledge that the possibility of coercion exists thereby undermines power. Such laxity encourages those who prefer not to obey the rules and discourages those who do. Sometimes an overly deferential chief executive refuses to use the legitimate power of the position, resulting in a common-law overlay to governance that limits the practical use of constitutional authority for successors. For positions that typically have too little inherent power, such a loss is unforgivable. Here is an example of an executive who gave away what his predecessors had fought to obtain:

> The governance documents of a college were in full accord with the guidelines of the American Association of University Professors: that is, they ceded appropriate curricular and peer-related matters to the faculty, but retained final authority for the president and the board. A new president, however, was persuaded by faculty leaders to establish an informal group of faculty advisors, a "kitchen cabinet," with whom he met frequently to review college policies and prospective actions. The result was that he had not only to follow all the rules of college governance, he also had to follow the advice of this inherently conservative group, whose members had their own, often contradictory, objectives. Were he to initiate an action not reviewed favorably by the kitchen cabinet, he would be accused of bad faith. Little change took place, and the president's successors were hamstrung by this additional layer of governance.

Although rewards tempt the inexperienced executive, their effect is limited. Few people are apt to receive a higher salary or status in the organization, or indeed a higher reward of any kind, than they truly believe they deserve. Many authorities today conclude that merit pay, for example, fails to alter performance. In my experience, almost without exception the best performers work skillfully and hard not for monetary reward but because they are driven to do so. They may deserve a raise and if so should receive it, but the raise will have little impact on future performance. The leader must be careful not to appear to believe that such rewards will cause these top performers to perform at an even higher level.

Much appreciation can come from the unexpected, nonmonetary reward—the note of thanks or sympathy, the extra word in the hall that reveals that the leader knows the individual, the postscript penned at the bottom of an otherwise routine letter, the pat on the back, literally or figuratively. Here is how one executive used this concept:

> The chief executive of a medium-sized nonprofit made a vow that each month she would write five staff members a personal, hand-written note of appreciation, encouragement, or sympathy. She asked her senior staff to suggest names and found that she never ran out. She learned a great deal about her staff; those who received the letters appreciated the trouble she took.

Influence

Influence can be symbolized by the statement "If you do X, Y will happen." The influential leader is in the role of counselor rather than commander, of predictor rather than guarantor. Influence of this sort is often based on *expertise* or prestige—specialized knowledge or achievement. The leader who is perceived as an expert obviously has a head start on acceptance for a program of change. However, the ability of the nonprofit executive to use expertise as the basis for leadership is complicated and grows more difficult with the size of the institution. It is especially hard for someone new on the job to demonstrate expertise, for several reasons.

For one thing, the new chief executive who is recruited from outside, even from the identical position at another, similar non-profit, may be an expert on some things but can hardly claim to be an expert on the new institution. Staff will believe that they know more, and at least for a while, many will be right. For a new executive to claim greater expertise would seem arrogant and foolish. One appointed from inside will be an expert on one part of the organization, but seldom on the whole.

Also, as a result of their training and experience, chief executives have technical proficiency in one field or another, but in their new position they generally are not called upon to provide that particular expertise. Instead, they are now presumed to be expert in the art of being a nonprofit chief executive. However, few have received the training that would allow them to claim such broad expertise.

Furthermore, overreliance on expertise can appear to force the executive down into the details, where God is said to dwell, but where the Devil may also be found. Henry Kissinger put it this way: "It is . . . the responsibility of the expert to operate the familiar and that of the leader to transcend it" (1982, p. 445).

Thus, the new nonprofit chief executive is in a quandary with regard to expert leadership. It will be tempting to try to project more mastery than one may really possess. On the other hand, to go too far in the other direction by professing ignorance will also result in failure, for then the chief executive will seem lacking in confidence or disingenuous. The most honest stance, and therefore the best, is to claim as much expertise as you honestly can and to show by example that you intend to become the leading expert, not on each part of the institution, but on the whole. Others may know more about the trees, but in time, no one will know more about the forest. Indeed, being able to view and understand an entire organization is one of the most rewarding aspects of being a chief executive.

Often staff, and sometimes trustees, believe that what they really need in their next leader is a recognized expert or scholar. This strategy often backfires, as in this example:

> The staff of a historical association with extensive research collections had gained the upper hand with the board and forced the departure of the chief executive, whom they had perceived as (only) a fundraiser. They insisted that the next director have a scholarly background; the board responded by hiring a professor from a nearby university who had done research at the association. First the board, and then the staff, came to realize that scholarly expertise had little to do with meeting the leadership needs of the association. Management and contributions both weakened; the director was fired and the association was soon involved in another search.

Some nonprofit executives serve as officers in a professional association, thus substituting status within the field for technical expertise. They become demonstrated experts on their profession on a national scale. This can be effective and a useful service as long as one is not away at professional meetings too much of the time.

Authority

To have the authority to say "Do X" and be obeyed without the threat of penalty or promise of reward requires that the leader be recognized as having the *legitimacy* to issue the command: legitimacy is a sine qua non of leadership. The legitimate authority of the nonprofit chief executive is established by the governance documents of the organization. The executive must be able to justify any action, especially those that may prove controversial, in light of those documents. The executive must understand both the legal structure of the organization and the evolution and state of its unwritten rules, which can be just as important. The authority of a chief executive also derives from, and is enhanced by, a search process that is consistent with organizational rules and norms. Otherwise, the chief executive can never claim to be fully legitimate. If the new leader has been appointed through a search that conformed to institutional standards, then even the most firmly antiadministration members of the staff are apt to be willing to give the leader a chance. Even they know that good leaders are needed, and they desire, or at least are willing, to be led by one (though they may have never met such a leader in person).

The role of the board, whose own actions and legal authority legitimize the leader, can be significant, as this example demonstrates:

The chair of the board of an arts organization insisted on having an office on the premises and the services of a secretary. He appeared once or twice a week for several hours, usurping the chief executive's secretary, and wandered the halls making inquiries and expressing opinions. Soon staff began to ignore the chief executive and to wait for the arrival of this highest authority. The institution lost direction, the chief executive left, but the board remained unwilling to stand up to the strong-willed chair.

In this case, the board chair was endowed with greater authority and employees had long deferred to him. Although the chief executive had been hired in a legitimate search, the greater legal authority and stature of the chair served to undermine the chief executive's ability to lead.

When authority is legitimized, it legitimizes the use of other strategies for shaping behavior and the application of the other sources of leadership. A leader who is legitimate can succeed, at least for a while, even if followers do not agree with the leader's decisions. The leader whose actions are illegitimate is headed for an early fall or by rights should be. Legitimacy is especially important in time of crisis, when the other sources of leadership may be less effective and when drastic action may be required.

But a moment's thought will show that so far this analysis is inadequate to explain the authority of leaders. For example, consider Jesus, Gandhi, and Martin Luther King, Jr. They rejected coercion and offered their followers no earthly rewards. Their effectiveness was not grounded in governance documents; they were not validated by a search process; their influence did not arise from expertise. Though opponents denounced them as illegitimate, followers viewed their legitimacy as emanating from a higher power: from God or from a just cause. Their authority originated in what Weber called *charisma*.

Although the word *charisma* originally referred to those who appeared to be divinely inspired, today charisma is said to apply to a wide range of public figures, ministers, politicians, actors, musicians, not all of whom are leaders in any sense and many of whom appear quite earthly. Although empirical research has shown that charismatic leadership is the most effective, some scholars distrust it. Drucker warns, "Beware Charisma!" (1989, p. 108), citing the harm done by charismatic leaders of the twentieth century—Hitler, Stalin, Mao—and the good work done by others who were less charismatic by most definitions: Truman, Adenauer, Eisenhower. (One might note, however, the difference between the way in which the first group of dictators, as contrasted with the second group of legitimately elected leaders, came to have power and the means they used to preserve it.)

Charisma is a hard word to pin down; its definitions have a certain mysteriousness and circularity. Some leaders have been great without charisma; others who were charismatic have attempted leadership but have failed. Gardner (1990, p. 35) said of the term *charisma*, "Its usefulness and appropriate definition remain in doubt." This suggests that the word has lost its usefulness and that another should be sought to replace it. Most treatments of leadership and charisma conclude that the principal effect of the charismatic leader is to inspire, particularly to inspire trust and confidence. *Webster's* second definition of *inspire* is "to exert an animating, enlivening, or exalting influence," which seems to capture well this aspect of leadership. We may not know the extent to which one can learn to be charismatic, and in its divine sense charisma is bestowed by God and cannot be learned. We can agree, however, that to have real influence, a leader must inspire followers. Therefore, a preferable term is *inspiration*.

Fisher (1991), distilling the work of many, concludes that four factors have the greatest influence on what I am calling inspirational leadership: personal style, perceived self-confidence, empathy, and social distance. The leader must become familiar with the four and decide how best to use them. For most of us, the last will prove particularly difficult.

1. *Style.* A leader should be perceived as an individual, true to him- or herself first, without undue concern as to what others may think. This is considered style. Can you recall a great leader who did not have one or more remarkably distinguishing traits that made

that leader identifiable and unforgettable? Maybe those traits had to do with dress, with voice, even with idiosyncrasies that one would not wish to find in a close friend or spouse. But above all, a leader's style is genuine and memorable. Style also refers to a leader's modus operandi. Some people prefer to "manage by walking around," others rarely leave their office. Some hold frequent staff meetings; others give marching orders only occasionally. Some are quite direct in their instructions to staff; others are more subtle. Without seeming affected, a leader must have a style that is distinctive: it is acceptable to appear eccentric as long as you really are. Be yourself.

2. *Perceived Self-Confidence.* Fisher (1991) calls not just for self-confidence, which is present on any list of the characteristics of leaders, but for *perceived* self-confidence. Followers must see and believe that the leader is supremely (but not foolishly) confident and regards failure as impossible and success as certain. Such confidence is contagious and inspiring. Certainly self-confidence is a characteristic that all great leaders have projected. Even in the darkest hours of World War II, Churchill was to be found in the streets of London, cigar in mouth and fingers in a "V." We know from their subsequent writings that great leaders had their moments of apprehension, but their doubt was not conveyed to their constituents. In projecting more confidence than they may feel, leaders are not being hypocritical or deceitful; rather, by showing their own optimism and resolve, they fulfill the principal obligation of a leader: to draw out even more from their followers than the followers thought they possessed.

3. *Empathy.* To be inspired, followers must be convinced that the leader understands them and the issues that affect them. This is essential when the leader is calling for sacrifice. The leader must be able to listen carefully, without interrupting, and be able to show through subsequent actions that the followers were heard and understood. Followers do not expect that the leader will always agree with them, but they do, and rightfully, expect to be heard. For

this reason, the effective chief executive will find ways of communicating with staff.

4. *Social Distance*. Social or psychological distance refers to a certain reserve that a leader must maintain, especially with those who report to the leader. Such a leader will be open but not intimate; friendly but not a friend; warm but not involved in the personal lives of subordinates; visible and well known but not familiar. Such a leader will always be a touch removed, finding friends and confidantes outside the organization. Unfortunately, this advice tends to be unwelcome among those who aspire to be nonprofit leaders.

At first, to seek to cultivate social distance seems dishonest, Machiavellian; having been trained from kindergarten not to seem aloof or remote, naturally we prefer to be liked. Had we acted otherwise on our way up, chances are we would not have been promoted to the point where becoming a chief executive is an option. After all, we tended to enter the nonprofit field because we like and care about people (Lynch, 1993). The findings of the research on leadership are clear, however: to be maximally effective, we must now unlearn some of the very lessons and discard some of the traits that got us where we are. While continuing to care about the people who work for our organization, we must now realize that our principal loyalty is to the organization itself, not to any individual person within it. As Lyman Bryson put it, "The qualities that get a man into power are not those that lead him, once established, to use power wisely" (quoted in Gardner and Reese, 1975, p. 204). It comes down to a choice between your personal desires and preferences—your human yearning to be liked—and the traits that will make you the most effective leader. If you are not willing to put the interests of your organization above your own wishes, in this way as in others, you will not be a maximally effective leader.

The concept of social distance may be difficult to accept, but it is perfectly logical. The better you know someone, the more that person's foibles and weaknesses become apparent. The more often you see a leader make mistakes or seem unsure, the less expert the leader appears and expertise as a source of inspirational leadership erodes. Just as a parent has more difficulty enforcing the rules as the children grow older and observe that the parent is fallible, so subordinates find it more difficult to follow the directions of a leader whom they know well. As they observe that the leader is all too human, they will naturally come to question the leader's wisdom, accuracy, and ultimately authority.

Remember that many people—teachers, ministers, physicians, police, and politicians—can earn our trust and respect without becoming our intimates. Indeed, an attempt at intimacy by such persons only engenders suspicion. Trust is based on evidence of trustworthiness; respect, on character and competence. Intimacy is a poor substitute for these.

The idea of social distance need not conflict with the importance of teamwork, which is essential for the success of any organization today. After all, teams have captains and coaches. Team members know that when they are well led, in the long run they and their institution will be better off. Fisher writes, "Among equals, there are no strong leaders" (1991, p. 16). Here is what can happen when the leader chooses merely to be an equal:

> A nonprofit chief executive operated exclusively on the teamwork model; all decisions and plans were made by consensus. The chief executive did not even aspire to be primus inter pares. The institution opened a new building with great expectations for attendance, only to find that it fell far short. (This has happened so many times in the nonprofit world as to have become almost the rule.) Staff size needed to be reduced, but the team found that without a strong leader, it was unable to make firm decisions about who should be retained and who let go. As attendance stalled and the budget problems worsened, the board replaced the executive.

The smaller the institution, the more difficult it may seem to maintain social distance. Yet Karen Simmons, director of the La

Salle University Nonprofit Management Development Center, having observed social distance being effective in an organization with
as few as two employees, argues that no organization is too small or
too service oriented for leadership to be enhanced by social
distance.

Some chief executives, especially those in human services, are
so uncomfortable in the role that unconsciously they try to strip
their position of its status. They attempt to handle their discomfort
by pretending that they are really no different than they were before
and certainly no better than anyone else. Often they use self-
deprecating humor, which can work if done skillfully but is liable
to backfire. The following two cases show the difficulties that arise
when a chief executive goes too far in revealing a level of discomfort with the position:

> An acting chief executive, in his first public appearance, made self-
> deprecating remarks. The chairman of the board told him, "Never run
> yourself down in public—it hurts the institution." He was eventually
> passed over for the permanent position.

> After a museum staff moved into a new building, one senior member
> complained to the director about her office. The director immediately
> offered to swap his larger quarters for hers. The editor, understand-
> ing that the position of director required certain perquisites even
> though the current occupant was willing to forgo them, wisely
> declined (Lynch, 1993).

Strange though it seems, distance produces fewer communication difficulties than does intimacy (Fisher, 1991). The explanation
may be that in a more formal relationship, matters are more apt to
be put in writing or stated more rigorously than if they are being
communicated orally between two friends.

A further reason for maintaining distance is to allow the executive to offer pointed but constructive criticism. Even the best staff member can improve, but the closer you are to your staff personally, the more difficult it is to criticize, even constructively. Of course, some staff members, rather than needing constructive criticism, deserve more severe action—up to and including dismissal. The more intimate you are with these individuals, the more difficult it is to do the right thing in such cases. Finally, it may be impossible.

As an experienced chief executive, I have yet to find an institution where my predecessor did not retain at least one senior staff member who should have been let go long before I got there. Usually the reason was that the executive had developed personal bonds with the staff member. But the chief executive is supposed to protect the interests of the organization, which do not always coincide with the interests of individuals who work there. When they do not, the ability of the executive to act on behalf of the organization must not be compromised.

The chief executive may become so close to certain members of the staff that they are viewed as the executive's favorites. Nothing will more quickly lead to disillusionment and poor performance than the sense by some senior staff members that others who are not performing as well are being treated better. The only stance by the chief executive that is right both in principle and in practice is to avoid becoming personally involved with senior staff members. Treat each the same: professionally.

Finally, a note of caution: there is obvious danger in being too distant, for then you run the risk of being seen as cold, remote, and uncaring (Fisher, 1991). Extended to an extreme, distance will be debilitating. Machiavelli wrote that it is better for the leader to be feared than loved, but both can be carried too far. To be respected is better than either. In the end, each nonprofit leader has to come to terms with the concept of social distance. Some may prefer to be somewhat less effective than to pay the price, but there seems no escaping that leadership will suffer.

Attributes of Leadership

Leadership stems from the sources just described and is given life by the attributes of individual leaders. Understanding of leadership has progressed to such a point that the characteristics that leaders tend to have in common can be described and therefore cultivated by the aspiring leader. Gardner (1990) draws on the extensive writings in this field and on his own experience to provide the following list of personal characteristics that contribute to leadership:

- Adaptability, flexibility of approach

- Ascendance, dominance, assertiveness

- Capacity to manage, decide, set priorities

- Capacity to motivate

- Capacity to win and hold trust

- Confidence

- Courage, resolution, steadiness

- Intelligence

- Judgment-in-action

- Need to achieve

- Physical vitality and stamina

- Skill in dealing with people

- Task competence

- Understanding of followers and their needs

- Willingness or eagerness to accept responsibilities

At first, this seems a daunting list. In actuality, it is less formidable than it appears, for all but three of these traits (dominance, intelligence, and the need to achieve) do not have to be genetic but can be learned or are naturally gained through experience. A drive toward dominance may be critical in some positions of leadership but is of less importance in the nonprofit sector, where persuasion rather than edict is the rule. Intelligence is a limiting factor in life, but someone who is under consideration for the position of chief executive or who has achieved the office has already met a certain standard. Scholarship has shown that leaders can actually be too able for those they would lead (Bass, 1990). A need to achieve must be present to some degree in anyone who has moved up through the ranks to be at or near the position of chief executive. It borders on a tautology to say that a chief executive must have a need to achieve; one who did not would have been weeded out long ago.

Why are physical vitality and stamina not largely inherent? First, without a sufficient amount of fitness and endurance, one could never have had the career success necessary to approach the position of chief executive in the first place. Second, as medical research shows ever more clearly, physical fitness and stamina can be developed and enhanced.

One trait from Gardner's set needs greater emphasis: resolution. One could argue that the single characteristic that all great leaders have shared is their resolve to succeed against adversity. The great leader perseveres, however long it takes and whatever the odds. Conversely, one who is not willing to fight for a valued principle or outcome is not apt to offer much in the way of leadership. Leaders believe, as Lynch (1993) puts it, that "As long as one is still trying, one has not failed. Giving up is thus the only way to fail" (p. 42).

Two attributes that are important in nonprofit leadership need to be added to Gardner's list: a sense of humor and risk taking. Having and expressing a sense of humor provides an indispensable stress-reliever both for leader and followers. The willingness to take risks is an absolute requirement, for no matter how carefully an organization and its leader have studied and planned, the future is sure to surprise. A leader who waits until near-certainty has been achieved before acting will have waited too long. Other organizations, more willing to take a chance, will have moved. The true leader is never so exhilarated and effective as when, after judicious thought and careful planning, the organization is led into a potentially great but risky new adventure. The person who fears taking a risk offers little promise of leadership. Browning captured the thought when he said, "A man's reach should exceed his grasp" (1962, p. 974).

Shakespeare told us that "Some are born great, some achieve greatness, and some have greatness thrust upon them" (*Twelfth Night*, 2.5.132). How these possibilities are to be applied to the great leaders is an eternal question for historians and students of leadership. It may be that the truly great leaders are born, though a careful reading of history and the early lives of, say, Winston Churchill, Ulysses S. Grant, Adolf Hitler (great in evil), and Harry Truman, would cast doubt on the thesis. But most of the characteristics of leadership listed above—which include all that are truly useful—can be cultivated. Even natural leaders draw on the sources of leadership authority and employ techniques that enhance their effectiveness, as the leader of any organization large or small can learn to do.

Acting Like a Leader

How should aspiring leaders behave to be most effective? How do they take advantage of the authority that comes with legitimate leadership, make the most of the leadership qualities that they possess, and use the forms of leadership, especially inspirational leadership, to maximum effect? Here are some important lessons:

- Keep the traditions of the organization constantly in mind and refer to them frequently. Remind everyone of the mission and provide a compelling vision of how the organization can and ought to be better. Reinterpret, in light of today's needs, the values for which it was founded and that establish the standard against which its actions must be measured.

- Use nothing less than the full power of the office of chief executive to create change within the style and governance of the organization. The adage "use it or lose it" applies to power, influence, and authority; the more you use, as long as you do so carefully, with full legitimacy, the more you will have (Lynch, 1993).

- Discuss change in particular cases rather than in the abstract; otherwise, the leader will be labeled as in favor of change for change's sake, undercutting effectiveness on issues that really matter. (Indeed, a case can be made for change for change's sake, but doing so openly will be counterproductive.)

- Never do, or allow to be done, anything that might compromise the legitimacy of the office. Not only will such actions reduce or even destroy your effectiveness but they will diminish the potential of the office for change and thus compromise your successors. Seek explicit ways to enhance its authority.

- Enhance the leadership abilities that you have and develop others. Build up your stamina and never compromise your integrity.

- Come to know your institution more broadly than anyone. For detailed knowledge, rely on others.

- Show your style.

- In public, always project at least as much confidence as you honestly can, even though it may be more than

you are feeling at the moment. You will be looking
ahead, taking the long view of the organization's
potential.

- Do not become too close to those who report to you.
  Without seeming cold, maintain a certain distance.

- Be able to laugh at yourself and the world.

- After judicious consideration, take a risk.

The fundamental objective for the leader of a nonprofit organization—indeed of any human endeavor—is to be an agent of change.

3

Starting Out Right

*All this will not be finished in the first one hundred
days. Nor will it be finished in the first one thousand
days, nor in the life of this administration, nor even
perhaps in our lifetime on this planet. But let us
begin.*

John Fitzgerald Kennedy, *quoted in
Theodore Sorensen's* Kennedy

Use the interval between leaving your old institution and arriving at the new one to catch up on your homework. Reread the most useful materials that you were sent and ask for more: budgets, financial reports, planning documents, salary information, résumés of your immediate staff, biographies of key trustees. Especially useful, because they were done by objective persons unconnected with the organization, are accreditation reports and institutional audits that are available in the larger organizations. After securing the permission of the person you will succeed, ask each senior staff member to send you a short report covering his or her area of responsibility. Make sure that they include an evaluation of the people who report to them. If you can, find out whether you will have to work with any disappointed internal candidates.

Plan your first few months in the new post with the view that the honeymoon should be used to get things done that would be more difficult later. What matters is not the duration of the honeymoon but its accomplishments. Unfortunately, many new chief executives, heady with their newfound power (some of which will prove illusory) and their new budgetary control, quickly make mistakes. A common one is to proceed at once to make major, visible expenditures on the chief executive's office or executive suite or on the institutional home if there is one. Many an executive has run into early difficulty over what was perceived as exorbitant spending on the new abode. Others have violated institutional norms by insisting that a family member, usually a spouse, be given an appointment at the organization. The following two examples show the risk of an early misuse of purse and power:

A major institution had for many years provided a house for its chief executive. A new appointee found the house to be in need of extensive repair and refurbishing and after arriving proceeded to have both done without securing the express permission of the board. An article in the local newspaper revealed that even though the institution had run a deficit for the last several years, $250,000 had been spent on these improvements. Community and trustee outrage rose to such a height that the new chief executive had to resign before his first year was up.

The spouse of a new chief executive had worked at the institution several years before his appointment and their marriage. Upon his arrival, he went to the head of his wife's former department to arrange for her to be reappointed, arguing that no search was necessary since her credentials had already been established and because during negotiations the trustees had promised that she would have such a post. The department head concurred. When this appointment was discovered, it was viewed as illegitimate, and even though she worked without salary, the protest brought the honeymoon to a quick end.

The impatient chief executive will move too quickly, before establishing credibility and learning the ways of the institution, bringing the honeymoon to a rapid end, as happened to this new executive:

> A nonprofit chief executive announced in his first month in office that staff salaries were significantly too low (by implication this oversight was the fault of his predecessor) and that he intended to increase them by 10 percent in the next budget year. Unfortunately, he had neglected to clear this plan with his financial officer and with board leaders. When it became impossible to deliver on his promise, his credibility fell and he soon departed.

At the opposite extreme from the impatient chief executive is the one whose main goal is to be liked and to remain in office as long as possible: Burns's (1978) "transactional leader." This leader believes that the way to extend the honeymoon is to make as few decisions as possible, none of which are controversial. Although it may not be apparent immediately, this chief executive will cause more suffering than the one who moves too rapidly. The rapid mover will soon depart, having provided the successor and the institution with a valuable lesson. The honeymoon-extender may be around for a long time, missing opportunities all the while.

How quickly the new executive should act depends on the needs of the institution. Gilmore (1988, p. 230) summarizes the disadvantages of moving too soon or too late. By taking major actions too early, you

- Do not yet fully understand the ramifications of a substantive issue, and therefore miss opportunities to do it right in one step without having to keep tinkering with it
- Miss political understandings
- Begin to muddy the waters so that you cannot differentiate between what is really going on and reactions to your initial moves

- Become isolated and encapsulated, losing allies that could have been developed, with more time and attention

- Get out in front of infrastructure, unable to sustain the change

By moving too slowly, you

- Miss a window of opportunity when people are looking to you for new directions, and therefore lose their support

- Build higher expectations that changes will be fully thought through, and are given less tolerance for mistakes

- Become socialized to the existing culture, no longer capable of being shocked by its practices or naive about potentially self-imposed limits

- Begin to own the status quo instead of being able to hold your predecessor responsible for it.

Gilmore (1988) summed it up this way: "The trick for the new leader is to link the growth of the learning curve with the decay of the honeymoon" (p. 230). By the time the honeymoon has waned, the stage for change should be well set.

The First Few Days

After years of waiting in the wings, at last you have your chance to be a chief executive. You are determined to hit the ground running and to make your first one hundred days as productive as those of FDR. However, you must temper your expectations. After all, FDR was an unusual man who presided during an unusual period of history, the Great Depression. No one since has had a first one hundred days like his; you certainly will not be the exception. JFK was closer to the mark when he asked for at least one thousand days.

Further, as someone, probably a former nonprofit chief executive, noted, "Responsibility always exceeds authority." As a new chief executive, you know that you have a great deal of responsibility; it will take time to determine how much authority goes with it and how best to exercise that authority. It is certain, however, that you will have less than absolute authority: whatever you are able to accomplish will come more from persuasion than command. Although Truman had a sign on his desk saying "The buck stops here," he also said "The principal power the president has is to bring people in and to try to persuade them to do what they ought to do without persuasion" (1965). You also need time to unearth the common law by which all institutions operate. Finally, all organizations have some long-term employees who prefer the status quo and who have outlasted several chief executives. It will take time to know who among them can be converted and who cannot. During these early days, as your aspirations are being tempered, remind yourself that you have come to the institution because you believe in its mission. Take the time and have the patience to meet and understand its people, all of whom have been there longer than you and some longer than you will ever be. Although many will offer their views on what is wrong with the organization and what to do about it, none will have the information, perspective, and responsibility that you have. You will need to discover the problems and opportunities for yourself. The way you go about it can help establish a platform for change:

- Meet with your senior staff team as early as you can, perhaps at breakfast your first day, to tell them in general terms what you expect of them and to describe your management style. A list of items is in Resource C.

- If you have not yet done so, meet early that first day with your senior assistant to explain your mode of operation.

- In your first two days in the new job, meet privately for an hour with each member of your senior staff to go over the reports that you requested of them. Ask questions and give them further assignments and follow-up.

- Carve out half of each day, for as many days as it takes, to walk the halls introducing yourself. Have a member of your staff who will be seen as neutral—perhaps your assistant—accompany and introduce you where appropriate. Say hello to everyone you meet, from the highest to the lowest. Be as visible as you can and let as many as possible see you and shake your hand. This will literally give you a firsthand feel for the people and space and will be deeply appreciated by all whom you meet and all who hear about it—and everyone will. Meeting you in this way will prove reassuring.

Remember too that in your first few weeks, everyone will be watching your slightest move, attempting to determine through the smallest details how you will handle larger matters, including those affecting them. "Even trivial issues will be spun into theories" (Gilmore, 1988, p. 133). The early rumors may defy belief, yet be repeated by otherwise sensible people, as at this institution:

A new chief executive was told that within his first week he had reportedly: (1) won the annual institutional footrace, (2) ordered the grass painted green (in order to mask the results of a lengthy drought), and (3) abolished the annual staff picnic. None was true.

The First Few Months

Once your initial introduction to the organization is well under way, you can turn your attention to establishing the work routine that fits your style. Here are some suggestions:

You will not succeed without a topflight executive assistant who works well with your preferred style. Unless you have brought your assistant with you, give your inherited assistant a few weeks to establish how well you can work together. Since this person is the senior secretary in the organization, it is reasonable to assume that he or she is at least competent, so level of skill is not apt to be the main issue. Rather, you need to have complete confidence that your assistant will be able to adapt to your work style rather than the other way around. The personal chemistry must be good; otherwise you will have to put up with a constant and eventually debilitating source of irritation. It is critical that your executive secretary not reveal confidences to anyone, especially your predecessor, and be loyal to you and you alone. If in the end you feel that you need someone else, given the length of service the person is apt to have, provide a generous early retirement or a transfer to another department. Here is a case that illustrates the problem:

> A new chief executive inherited the assistant who had served her predecessor for fifteen years. She observed that relations with the assistant seemed to be strained but had no idea why. She discovered that the assistant was upset at the new chief executive's different way of doing things and that on the assistant's route home from work, she often stopped by the home of the predecessor to complain. The predecessor made sure that these complaints reached the ears of key staff and trustees. The executive gave the assistant a generous early retirement package, but considerable damage had already been done.

Branch out and expand your contacts. By the end of the first month, you should have met many of the groups that make up the institution. As soon as you can arrange it, meet privately and individually with the leadership of your board, certainly with the members of the executive committee. Like you, they are busy, but they will appreciate your making the effort to spend time with them early in your tenure. Ask these board leaders for their suggestions, not only regarding the organization but also regarding the board itself. Find out why they serve on the board. As Herman and Heimovics (1991, p. 107) recommend, look for a "champion of change"—a board member who is dissatisfied with the status quo and sees how the organization can become distinctly better. You should also meet with those outside the organization—foundation officers, for example—whose support you will need.

Meet once with each major committee or department. These groups will present you with their agenda and grievances, but since it is early in your tenure, all they will really expect is that you listen. You will learn a great deal and begin to attach names to faces.

Attend as many functions as you can. You will not be expected to stay long and everyone will be grateful that you showed up at all. Your goal is to meet as many people as possible and to be seen as already involved in the life of the organization. Take your staff on a half-day or all-day retreat, perhaps to work on a SWOT analysis (see Chapter Six). This is a good way to size them up individually and as a team and to learn a great deal about the organization in the process. Look for some important but small victories, ones that can be implemented without calling attention to themselves. Keep in mind that intermediate degrees of change produce almost as much resistance as larger ones. When the time is right, therefore, "it is often better to go for all the change one wants . . . because the amount of flak may reach a plateau" (Gilmore, 1988, p. 243).

As the months of your first year go by, the institution will become increasingly familiar. One day, you will suddenly feel as though you belong (it is important to realize, however, that some old-timers may not see it that way). Remember that while you have an investment in change, most of those with whom you work do not.

After the problems and opportunities presented by the organization have come into focus, lay out a set of three to five major goals for the rest of your first year. Revise this list at least annually. Continue to reassess and evaluate, looking back to see which objectives you have accomplished and which you have not, and see if you can understand why.

Your Predecessor

There is a tide in the affairs of institutions: when a new stage in the cycle arrives, a new leader with a new and different set of abilities should be, and usually is, chosen. But this tends to make conflict between the old and the new an inevitable by-product of the cycle of succession. Most predecessors and their supporters are soon apt to become offended by some act of the successor; how could it be otherwise? Here is a particularly egregious example:

> The founding director of a historical society finally reached retirement age. His replacement discovered that in the interval between his appointment and arrival, the outgoing director had made his spouse a vice president of the society, added several new staff, and awarded large salary increases. The new director also learned that, unbeknownst to the board, the society had been running a deficit for several years, which increased significantly due to the new expenditures. The new director soon began to meet resistance not only from the now-ensconced spouse of the former director but from other senior staff members as well. Soon the chair called to tell him that things were not working out and that he should resign immediately. It took the threat of a lawsuit for the departing new director to receive a fair severance package. Later he discovered that the predecessor and spouse had been entertaining staff members at their home, plotting his departure. A capable man, he landed on his feet and soon had an excellent position at the opposite end of the country. The board of the society elected a new chair and used a professional search consultant to help locate their next director.

Many searches and the operations of many boards have not been managed professionally until recently; similarly, few boards have dealt adequately with the problem of the predecessor. A far-sighted, responsible board, aware of the inherent conflict, will ensure that the predecessor is absent for at least a year, but such boards are rare. All too often, the predecessor is nearby, sometimes only blocks away and even a frequent visitor to the institution. One incoming college president found that for five years, his predecessor, who had been given an office on campus, continued to come to the president's office to pick up his mail. Another chief executive, assured that his predecessor would have long departed, found him ensconced in an office across the hall. A third learned after his departure that the predecessor had continued to entertain key trustees and staff at dinner parties whose principal subject of conversation was—guess who?

In some cases, the predecessor remains on the board. Given the ego of most chief executives and the relationship that a good chief executive builds up with the board over time, this is usually a recipe for an ineffective succession. One predecessor who remained a board member marked up confidential minutes of trustee meetings, identifying perceived slurs and criticisms, and sent them to staff confidantes.

A predecessor who has held office for a number of years will have had a key role in the selection of most members of the board. Many will have a loyalty to the predecessor that exceeds their feelings toward the institution and certainly toward the new chief executive. The agenda for change of the new chief executive will be seen by some trustees and by most predecessors as an implicit criticism. While you are a finalist, ask whether the predecessor will have an office at the institution and a seat on the board. If the answer to one or both is yes, the job may be compromised beyond repair. Let someone else be the guinea pig.

Of course, these problems should not exist in the first place. After all, a board of trustees, as the title reflects, and any governing board regardless of name, is entrusted with the protection of the interests of the institution in perpetuity. This duty transcends all others, certainly including loyalty to one individual. A few simple rules would allow boards to meet this solemn responsibility. Boards should

- Express appreciation publicly for the work of the outgoing chief executive and then turn their attention and loyalty to the institution and their commitment to the successor.

- Provide the outgoing chief executive with a paid sabbatical leave (at larger institutions) and require that it be taken elsewhere. If the outgoing chief executive is too young to retire, the board should assist the executive in finding another position.

- Adopt a policy stating that once a chief executive has resigned or retired, membership on the board is concluded. Do not send minutes and institutional papers to the predecessor or provide him or her with an office at the institution.

- Confront a predecessor, if necessary, who is acting irresponsibly and ask that the behavior cease. The board cannot expect the new executive to do so; it is a board responsibility. The knowledge that board members, whose respect and assistance the predecessor will wish to have, are aware of the shenanigans may be all that is required to ensure that they stop.

Meanwhile, if your case is typical, none of these steps will have been taken. Instead, it is going to be up to you to manage your predecessor as best you can. I urge you to reach out, no matter what impression you have. Meet for lunch occasionally, at least for a year or two. You will learn some useful things, and, if nothing else, you and your predecessor will see each other as human beings who despite differing styles have the good of the institution at heart. It cannot hurt and may help. It is surprising how much good it can do to ask for advice even if you do not act on it.

Even a faultless predecessor—in fact, especially a faultless predecessor—may provide you with a problem: senior staff may be unable to transfer their loyalty, as happened at this agency:

> A new executive director's inherited staff included a man dedicated to the previous executive director (who had been fired), and this staff person found every opportunity to challenge her. Eventually, the discontent spread, producing a loss of teamwork and a breakdown in authority. The executive sent the man a written warning, citing examples of inappropriate behavior, which in response grew even worse. Sensing that not only her authority but her survival in the position were being challenged, she sent a second and much more stern final warning. When her challenger saw that she intended to fight and to use all the power of her office, he suddenly resigned.

Stress

No one should become a chief executive without being aware of the increased level of stress that will result. There is simply no doubt that the chief executive's job is the most stressful in the organization, in part because of the volume of work to be done and the number of meetings to attend. The hours are long and the job is wearing; one becomes physically and mentally tired. But the chief executive's position is different not just in degree but in kind.

For example, as Truman noted, the buck stops on the chief executive's desk: when you cannot solve a problem, there is no higher authority to whom you turn. Now and again you can and should ask your board chair for advice, but if it happens too often, you invite micromanagement and a loss of confidence. After all, the board has a chief executive to identify problems and their solutions without having to be directly and regularly involved.

In addition, chief executives are dismissed routinely with little or no notice and in the absence of anything like a fair evaluation. Living with the knowledge that at any moment the boom can be lowered is stressful.

A chief executive was in his sixth year at an institution that had been suffering attendance declines. He was contacted by a search consultant and heavily recruited by a similar institution in another city, eventually becoming a finalist there. Although he and his family were sorely tempted, the chair of the board of his institution told him that they wanted him to stay and gave him a positive evaluation and a salary increase. These, together with the sense that he was truly needed where he was, led to him to withdraw as a candidate. Three months later, the board chair, after consulting with other board members by telephone (rather than calling a meeting as was required by the bylaws) informed him that he was fired.

Other stress-inducing factors are the following:

Uprooting. A chief executive years from retirement is not apt to retire in the current position and is therefore the one member of the organization least likely to remain with it or in the community in which it is located. As the new chief executive and family are putting down roots, they cannot help but be aware that someday perhaps unexpectedly the family will have to be uprooted.

Full responsibility. The future of the organization rests more on the performance of the chief executive than on that of any other single individual and the chief executive knows it. "Uneasy lies the head that wears a crown" (*Henry IV, Part II*, 3.1.31). The chief executive is the most obvious target for blame when things go wrong. Consequently, do not worry too much when you receive credit that you may not fully deserve.

Lonely at the top. The chief executive may have to fire senior persons who have been at the institution longer and who are in some cases respected greatly by other staff members. They and their families will never forgive you. Therefore, as discussed in Chapter Two, a wise executive will not develop close personal friendships among the senior staff. But if you work hard, have little time for socializing outside your job, and find it difficult to develop friends in the workplace, you may indeed wind up with few friends or none. It is lonely at the top.

Unappreciated success. As noted, an inevitable task of the new chief executive is to undo some of what the predecessor accomplished: a favorite vice president must be fired; a policy must be altered or scrapped. In some cases, the new chief executive is able to quickly accomplish a goal that the predecessor could not. Few predecessors will be entirely happy about such developments; neither may some of their supporters among trustees and staff. The activist must walk the tightrope of trying to be a change agent while not incurring the enmity of those who have made some of the changes especially necessary.

Always "on." The chief executive is always on stage or waiting in the wings to be called on at a moment's notice. In almost every setting, the chief executive is expected to be present, to be charming, leaderly, and able to answer on the spur of the moment any conceivable question.

Measuring success. Success at leading a mission-oriented nonprofit, which has no bottom line, is difficult to define and to demonstrate. Often success seems to be in the eye of the beholder—in this case, the board. Trustees and others will claim that they know how to recognize a successful chief executive, but they will not necessarily be correct. Often the external and more visible aspects of leadership will be unduly emphasized while more important ones go unnoticed and unappreciated. (This is why the chief executive should take a prominent role in defining what would constitute a successful performance.)

In short, the job of chief executive includes long hours, has enormous responsibility without concomitant authority, makes friendships hard to come by and success difficult to define, and has little job security. Given all the stress that this set of conditions can produce, it is imperative that each chief executive find some method of stress relief and practice it faithfully.

Gardner quotes Lord Moran, "Men of good will saddled with the fate of others need great courage to be idle when only rest can clear their fuddled wits" (1990, p. 134), and observes that the stress management techniques of the leaders he has known have one thing in common: they are nonverbal, involving such activities as music, reading, and sports. Churchill's painting is perhaps the best example. (I recall one of my most relaxing days, in which the only words I spoke were to wish long life to a released cutthroat trout!)

Medical evidence indicates that one form of nonverbal activity, exercise, is the single best stress-reducer, and of course it has other benefits as well: lower weight, higher cardiovascular fitness, and stamina. Get regular exercise and you will be a better person on the job and off it and live longer. To ensure that your stress-relief program is not bumped by your official duties, schedule your exercise or other stress reduction method and follow that schedule slavishly. Enter your exercise appointments into your daily calendar and adhere to them.

If it suits you, and many find it necessary especially for writing projects, work at home part of the time. Since some people (your board chair?) are prejudiced against an executive who works at home, have an extension set up so that calls to your office can be seamlessly transferred to your home. Remind your assistant not to say, "He (or she) is working at home today." Use a modem on your home computer to connect to the office electronic mail system (and the world).

While you are engaged in the job, find ways to make it more enjoyable. Decorate and personalize your office as you wish (but be frugal). Provide such accoutrements as give you pleasure. Enjoy the new people that you meet, and entertain appropriately. Avoid treating the institution and your position in it as a life or death matter. Do your best, then go home and relax. Spend some time with your family or friends; pet your dog.

Attend professional conferences and get to know your colleagues. While avoiding the penthouse suite, make your travel for the institution as agreeable as possible. Join a frequent flier club and upgrade to first class (at your own expense). Rent a mid-sized car rather than a compact. Dress well if it makes you feel better and you can afford it.

Try to develop a friendship with at least one other chief executive, someone you can trust. Get together off-site with your friend to share "war stories" and for mutual support. Form a small group of peers who can meet informally once or twice a year, perhaps at the time of a professional association meeting, for this same purpose. Here are two examples of how such collegiality worked to good effect:

The new chief executive of a small service agency had been promoted from within. She was highly motivated, but had never had the opportunity to learn how to manage and to lead an organization. She struggled for months, burning the midnight oil and herself nearly out, but found herself confronting leadership problems that merely working harder or longer could not solve. Recognizing that she needed to learn from others, through the local umbrella organization of nonprofits in her city, she got in touch with executives from several smaller nonprofits. As she grew more comfortable and trusting, she began to ask them for advice. Soon she had half a dozen colleagues whom she could call and consult about almost any problem she was facing. Some of her closest friends emerged from this group.

Two chief executives in cities an hour apart met halfway in between for lunch on alternate months. They found it a godsend not to be on stage, not to have to impress, and not to have to hide their professional and personal problems for fear of appearing weak.

In times of particular stress, it may be wise to seek professional counseling. Psychologists who specialize in executive stress can be found in every city.

The most important advice that this book offers is this: find your method of stress relief and make it your highest priority. You will be more effective in your job, you will be a happier person in the office and at home, you will have more years of productivity, and you will live longer. What else offers so much reward for the effort? Goethe (1912, p. 244) said it best: "One ought, every day at least, to hear a little song, read a good poem, see a fine picture, and, if it were possible, to speak a few reasonable words."

Part II

· ·

Building Blocks of Effective Leadership

Of course, a chief executive who is not an effective administrator will succeed at nothing; not even the short-term, day-to-day activities will be done well, and time will not be available for the vital, change-oriented leadership tasks that only the chief executive can perform. Many techniques exist to minimize the time spent on routine tasks and to maximize time available for the most important ones.

At their worst, meetings not only waste large amounts of time, they undercut the authority of the chief executive. But since meetings are the vehicle by which much institutional business gets done, their conduct can determine the rate and extent of change. A little common sense and discipline can go a long way toward making them a boon rather than a drag on you and the organization.

Delegation is a key management skill that strengthens people and organizations. By delegating effectively, you can ensure that an expert management team is developed that can carry on your changes even after you leave.

Information technology has changed the way people work and will soon change the way they learn and live. Organizations that fail to take advantage of its benefits will surely fall behind. No effective, modern chief executive can remain personally ignorant of the benefits of the information revolution. No change-oriented chief executive will allow control over this vital tool to pass to someone else in the organization.

The chief executive must master many administrative and leadership tasks, but a few are critical if the executive is to be an agent of change. Perhaps the most important is assembling the best senior management team that the executive can find and that the organization can afford. The aphorism "He who hesitates is lost" can well apply to the chief executive who waits too long to assemble a top-flight senior team. With the wrong team, you have no hope of being an agent of change; with the right one, it is hard not to be. The trustees to whom you report and the senior staff whom you decide to retain know that leaders can be judged by the quality of the people they hire. After all, change does not arise solely from the will and the actions of the chief executive; rather, the work of a well-led team is required. The team must consist of members who are intelligent, hardworking, loyal, and who will adopt an empathetic chief executive's agenda as their own. If you find such a team waiting for you upon your arrival, count your lucky stars. Most often you will have to create it by releasing some, retraining others, and hiring new members.

A second indispensable element for the agent of change is mastery of the institutional budget. In the end, the important decisions and plans of an institution are revealed and implemented in the way in which it decides to spend its money. It is not much of an oversimplification to say, "What is not in the budget does not matter." The first task of the new chief executive is to ensure that the budget is in balance; the second is to use it to foster the agenda for change. Broad agreement should exist between what the institution says about itself through its mission statement and other documents and what the budget reflects. The chief executive must understand the budget broadly and have a trustworthy financial officer who understands it in the finest detail. Final authority over the institutional budget must never be relinquished.

At most institutions, the largest element in the expenditure budget is staff salaries and benefits. Except for a few scoundrels, some recently exposed, no one enters the nonprofit sector primarily to make money. Yet those in the sector naturally expect to be treated fairly and to receive as much reward for good service as the institutional budget will permit. Human nature being what it is, salary increases seldom cause a visible improvement in morale. But surely the system can be made fair, can be explained clearly, and can reward those who work most effectively in the direction of the institutional vision.

As the budget is the key short-term vehicle for change, so the institutional plan is the key long-term instrument. Not even the most moss-bound conservative will openly deny the need to have a plan and therefore the need for planning. Yet to be engaged in planning is not only to have accepted that change is inevitable, it is to have moved on to a discussion of which changes and when—and that is a long step in the right direction. Thus, planning offers an important way to shift attitudes and to narrow the ground of those who choose not to see beyond the status quo. Today, planning is often integrated with quality management. Done correctly, the two complement each other.

Nonprofits are mission-driven; their raison d'être is to fulfill the objectives for which they were chartered. But the mission has no bottom line by which it can be assessed. The only way an institution can know to what extent it is fulfilling its mission is to evaluate its program offerings and administrative operations rigorously. Most institutions have room for improvement in determining the impact of their activities and the extent to which they are fulfilling their missions. Good intentions and promising activities are not a sufficient substitute for careful evaluation.

4

Using Time and Technology as Tools

We must use time as a tool, not as a couch.
John Fitzgerald Kennedy

On the way to becoming a chief executive, you have learned to become a good administrator: to keep up with paperwork, to be punctual, to meet deadlines. However, the chief executive not only has the most complex set of administrative tasks of anyone at the organization, the executive also carries an additional set of time-consuming but vital duties that no one else has the authority, responsibility, or perspective to carry out. To leave enough time for them you must become an even better administrator.

The first task is to manage your time—your most precious resource—and your office in the most efficient way possible. Many techniques and devices are available to help the chief executive do so. A second necessity is to avoid wasting time at meetings and to make those that you do attend productive. A third is to use the key tool of the successful executive: delegation. A fourth, most important to the institution as a whole, is to use information technology to enhance productivity and quality. In each of the four, the executive can not only increase efficiency and productivity but also set a good example for staff.

Managing Your Time for Efficiency

Behind every successful administrator is an excellent assistant who has adapted to the executive's work style and who filters the work load, wards off those who would use up time unproductively, and helps to decide priorities. With that person in place, the leader can use many techniques to gain efficiency and free up time for leadership activities. Here are several suggestions:

1. Bennis (1973) warned of the unconscious conspiracy of urgent but minor matters that, unless the new chief executive is careful, will override leadership activities. To avoid such a problem, rank the tasks that confront you and spend the majority of your time on the most important. Lynch (1993, p. 13) suggests separating your tasks into four groups: (1) urgent, high payoff, (2) not urgent, high payoff, (3) urgent, low payoff, and (4) not urgent, low payoff (often simply deferring an item in this last category will reveal it as unnecessary). He notes that the true leadership activities fall into category 2: those that do not have to be done immediately but which when done have a large impact. Try to find and focus on these tasks and on the urgent, high-payoff tasks that no one else can handle. When you do turn to an urgent task, complete it promptly. Be sure that you do not end a week with several urgent tasks begun but none completed.

2. Force yourself to handle each item that crosses your desk only once, making minor decisions immediately. This requires that you have the discipline to decide and to act; if you cannot do so even with routine business, you will not be a successful chief executive. Of course you will make a few misjudgments, but you will improve and the time you save will more than offset them.

3. Do a good job with your internal correspondence but do not strive for perfection; routine memos and letters do not require it. Remember Voltaire's well-known admonition that the best is the enemy of the good. Save time for those matters where your absolute

best will make a difference. (For example, since few internal items require a formal response, write your reply on the incoming document, have it copied and the copy sent back to the sender.)

4. If you can do it well, dictate (but remember that it is harder than it seems and requires an assistant who is able to improve your spoken prose). If you are set up to do so, type drafts of correspondence on your computer and send them to your assistant over your local area network for polishing and production.

5. Use a "to do" list. Have your assistant type each day's schedule on a three by five card and carry it for quick reference.

6. When meeting one-on-one, do so in the other person's office. This has several advantages: it gets you out and around, giving you a valuable perspective and keeping you in better touch with your constituents; people are more relaxed when you meet them in their surroundings; you are apt to understand them better and to learn more; you seem less domineering and less interested in control. When your business is concluded, you may rise and leave—you do not have to worry about how to extricate the person from your office.

7. Be punctual and cancel only in an emergency. Unless everyone among your senior staff learns these habits, the group as a whole cannot manage its time well, for some will always be wasting their time waiting for others. These practices must start at the top. Lead by example.

8. Learn to say no gracefully but effectively. As chief executive, you will be much in demand. The sponsors of most organizational functions will want you to attend. In a large percentage of these cases, your presence may be hoped for but is not really expected; many invitations are extended merely to keep you informed. At some of the events you do attend, you need only put in an appearance. Fisher (1984) describes how the busy chief executive can enter, say hello and shake a few hands, or make a few remarks if asked, and then move on, presumably to the next event of the evening. Only you need to know where you are headed—which

could be, and sometimes should be, home to stretch out with a good book.

Making Meetings Productive

For better or worse, organizations now conduct their affairs through meetings. Most appear to have adopted the motto "When in doubt, form a committee and call a meeting." Yet few stop to ask whether so many meetings are truly necessary and if so, how they can be made more efficient. Cohen and March (1986) report that academic presidents spend half their time in meetings; I would not be surprised if the average for all nonprofit chief executives were higher. Yet experienced chief executives tend to be dubious, if not downright negative, about the cost/benefit ratio of meetings. Fisher (1984) writes that "the more committee meetings you attend, the less effective you are" (p. 90). With the exception of a few key, high-level committees, you cannot attend routine committee meetings and still expect to accomplish all that a chief executive needs to accomplish. If you must attend them, you should chair them.

Beyond the time taken, meetings present a dilemma: unless they are handled with care and with a firm hand, they tend to make the executive, in appearance if not in fact, subject to a democratic process. To be present at a meeting, whether in the chair or not, politely listening to the discussion and observing the arrival of consensus, appears to obligate the executive to agree. But in most cases, presiding over consensus is not all that governance documents—even academic ones—expect of the chief executive. Thus, when the executive does attend a meeting, it is important that the ground rules be clear. Here is an example in which the chief executive had to clarify the rules:

The director of a small museum met with her senior staff weekly, one member of whom tended to take charge. The director noticed that this staff member, after introducing an appropriate topic, would often conduct a straw poll to ascertain the opinion of the group, even in regard to matters that were clearly the prerogative of the director. Eventually, the director had to remind everyone that the purpose of these meetings was not to make group decisions but to provide her with advice.

Some meetings are vital both to the institution and to the chief executive's career. The group upon whom the chief executive's future most depends is the board, and most trustees observe the chief executive exclusively during meetings of the board. When you walk into a board meeting as chief executive, you are being presented with the only opportunity you may have to impress the majority of trustees. If these meetings appear to be unplanned and are unproductive, most trustees will conclude that is the way the executive conducts all business. The tone set by the chief executive in meetings with the senior staff is also critical. If these meetings are poorly run, you set a bad example and undermine the staff's confidence in you.

Since, like television, meetings are here to stay, our only option is to improve them. To do so is much easier than the prevalence of unproductive meetings would suggest. All it takes is planning and discipline.

Planning

Some meetings are called for the specific purpose of taking an action; others are informational, called to communicate; some are a combination. The focus here is on meetings whose aim is to conduct business, to take action, although much of this advice applies to any kind of meeting.

Too many meetings take place with little planning or forethought. Each of us has attended meetings whose exact purpose no one present can remember or describe, often leading to a kind of "Alphonse-Gaston" repartee, or meetings when the chair said, "Here we are again at our weekly meeting. What shall we talk about today?" Nevertheless, few of these meetings adjourn for lack of an agenda. Parkinson (1957), who must have attended many meetings, said that work expands to fill the time available. If he had said that talk expands, that would explain why meetings seldom end early.

For an organization to succeed, every function must have a person with the responsibility and authority for carrying it out; that person must be clearly identified and held accountable. This rule applies from the loftiest trustee action on down. Thus, for every meeting, someone must have the responsibility and authority for the work that needs to be done before, during, and after and be held accountable for its success. That person is the chair, perhaps assisted by the secretary.

Prior to the meeting, the chair should ask the following questions:

Is the meeting truly necessary? Is it the best use of the time of the attendees? Or is it merely a regularly scheduled meeting without an agenda or action items to be considered? If the meeting requires travel by one or more of the attendees, could it not be accomplished through a telephone conference call? (Although such calls are not as effective as face-to-face meetings, the travel time saved may be worth it.)

Can the meeting be abolished? If it has been canceled more than once, it may be possible. If not, does it have to meet so often?

Must the meeting last so long? How often have we attended a meeting that was scheduled to last for two hours, only to have the first hour and a half wasted and all the business miraculously concluded in the last half hour? Would such a meeting have accomplished less if it had met for an hour (or, dare I say it, for half an hour)? Some chief executives are said to conduct their meetings standing!

Who really must attend the meeting? Scholarship, ignored by virtually all (especially scholars who attend meetings), and common sense show that meetings called for action are most productive when attended by a small number (the ideal being between six and eight). It is human nature, however, to think that the more who attend, the more who can contribute or at least become informed. But this is the precise attitude that makes meetings accomplish so much less than they could. If too many are present, those who have something important to contribute will have less time in which to do so and those who are senior, observing that they are not with their peers alone, may remain silent. As long as no key person is excluded, a smaller group will get more done. Therefore, exclude anyone who cannot participate as an equal as well as anyone who might be there only to receive information that can be imparted in some other way.

When these tough rules are initially implemented, those who are left out for the first time will be hurt. But if it is explained carefully that a meeting is being held not for the purpose of communicating but for taking action, and if a full program of communication is present, most will accept it and be glad for the extra time. After all, they too know how much time is wasted in unproductive meetings.

Chairing

Once time, date, and attendees are selected, the chair should send out the agenda for the meeting, far enough in advance to allow time for those attending to complete premeeting tasks. When possible, distribute important documents or reports in advance. The object is to do everything possible to ensure that the maximum amount of time at the meeting can be spent thinking, debating, and acting. The chair should ask for suggested changes in the agenda and once they are received decide which to accept. An astute chair will consent to all that do not compromise the chair's ability to achieve the desired outcome from the meeting. This is another important point: except for elected and parliamentary bodies, the chair should know exactly what should come out of the meeting and do everything fair to bring it about. The chair who has no idea what should emerge, or who, anxious to be fair, bends over backward so far that nothing is accomplished, should not be chairing meetings. Secretly, at least, most of those present will thank the chair for taking charge.

The chair and others attending might wish to take the time to put in writing any important statements that they plan to make at the meeting. These should be brief enough to be read aloud. The discipline of writing out a statement, knowing it will be read, will improve its clarity.

Meetings that are regularly scheduled should take place at a time and in a setting conducive to action: at some time other than late in the afternoon and in a comfortable room with windows, natural light, a good supply of air, and a prominent and accurate clock.

If these guidelines have been followed, the stage is set for a meeting at which the maximum amount of work can be accomplished in the minimum amount of time. Whether this actually happens depends on how the chair and the attendees conduct themselves. Here are some ground rules for the chair:

Start the meeting precisely on time. Wait for no one. Those who are habitually late will soon discover that they have missed out on important matters. If minutes need to be taken (if you are not certain, see that they are), have it done by someone other than a member of the committee. It is impossible to take minutes and be a full participant and no one should be called upon to make the sacrifice. Every organization has at least one confidential secretary who can take minutes.

Review the agenda. However, assuming that it has been available for a few days, do not invite changes. Then explain the purpose of the meeting. If it is the first meeting of the committee, or if many new members are present, review the points made in the section below that describe how participants should conduct themselves to make meetings successful. Be especially clear about confidentiality. Describe how you intend to conduct the meetings of the group.

Have high expectations of each participant. If you are disappointed, offer constructive criticism later.

Keep the discussion moving toward action. Ideally, you will have the authority to gently silence someone who is too long-winded or who is making the same point for the second or third time. Periodically, you should sum up where you think the discussion has led. Always be on the lookout for a consensus or a natural moment when the group is ready for a vote or has exhausted the issue and needs to move on. Suggest whichever you sense is appropriate.

Take action. Make sure that action is taken on each item on the agenda.

Adjourn the meeting. End earlier than scheduled and never later. This will encourage brevity and action.

Attending

The chair can only do so much: the success of a meeting depends at least as much on how the participants conduct themselves. Here are some premeeting suggestions for attendees:

- Notify the chair if you have an objection to the agenda and the secretary if you have a correction for the minutes.

- Read all the pertinent materials and think about them. If the matter is important, put your thoughts in writing. Discuss the nonconfidential items with colleagues.

- Make a tentative decision about your position on each agenda item.

- Show up on time or even a little early.

During the meeting itself:

- Listen carefully to your colleagues: *be there.* Do not spend your time planning eloquent remarks or daydreaming. Think before you speak and raise your hand to be recognized. Make your points only once, succinctly.

- Read any brief written statements aloud rather than handing them out. Observing that if you have gone to the trouble to prepare your statement in advance and to read it, other attendees are apt to pay more attention.

- Accept the decision of the majority and do not discuss confidential matters outside the committee meeting. Beware your skillful associates who can deduce what took place by your body language or by what you do not say in response to their questions.

If these steps are followed by all parties, meetings can be productive and even enjoyable.

Delegating: A Key Management Skill

Coolidge said, "In the discharge of the duties of the office, there is one rule of action more important than all others. It consists of never doing anything that someone else can do for you" (1929, p. 196). At first, this advice sounds autocratic, even despotic. Not so: unless you delegate, you cannot lead; it is that simple. Fisher makes the point this way: "Delegate everything but final authority" (1984, p. 90). Jenks and Kelly (1985) have an excellent discussion of delegation.

Delegation is vital because even at a small organization, or perhaps especially there, more tasks arrive on the chief executive's desk than even the most hardworking person could handle alone. The executive who attempts to manage them all personally will not have enough time for those that no one else can complete, of which there are always more than enough. After all, the reason an organization has a chief executive is because a particular set of critical responsibilities falls to that position and to none other. Furthermore, presumably the reason you became a chief executive is because you already mastered the skills required for lower-level positions and were ready to tackle a set of higher-level ones.

Here are examples of responsibilities that fall only to the chief executive:

- Receiving gifts. When major donors give, they want to look the chief executive in the eye.

- Interaction with the board. The board, collectively and individually, expects direct contact with the chief executive.

- Financial management, planning, and quality improvement. These tasks need to be visibly led by the chief executive.

- Recruitment, evaluation, and advancement of senior staff. To do these well takes time.

- Appearance at certain public occasions.

However, the most important task of the chief executive and the one that no one else can do, though many can help, is simply to think long and hard about the organization and its future. No one else has the breadth of view and the responsibility to raise the great institutional questions.

Unfortunately, tasks of low payoff (Bennis's "unconscious conspiracy") can eat up so much time that too little is left for long-range planning. As has been shown time and again in the corporate world, this is disastrous to the future of organizations. There are many companies whose leaders failed to take time to think and to understand the broad movements going on in society; as a result, these companies lost market share or disappeared.

Thus, the chief executive simply has no choice but to use every means available to free up the time to think. Delegation is one of the chief executive's most important tools. Without it, you cannot lead and your organization cannot thrive.

It is tempting for the chief executives of smaller nonprofits to believe that there is no one to whom to delegate. If that is your belief, make sure that you are not merely rationalizing your own unwillingness; after all, any organization with more than one employee has a potential delegator and delegatee. If it is true that you have no one to whom any tasks can be delegated, your top priority should be to hire such a person or, failing that, to get an intern, to recruit more volunteers, or to call more often on board members.

Benefits of Delegation

Delegation is essential to the growing, idea-based organization and vital to the development of those who report to the chief executive (and to the people who report to them, all the way down the ladder). One can paraphrase Coolidge by saying that a vice president should never do something that a director could do, a director should never do something that a manager could do, and so on down to the positions that have no one to whom to delegate. When the chief executive delegates (and by analogy when vice presidents delegate to directors, and so on), many benefits accrue:

Motivation. Although some of what is delegated is routine, delegatees find themselves working in new areas and learning new things. Most rise to the occasion and overall performance and job satisfaction increase. Tasks go to those who have the optimum balance of ability, available time, and motivation.

Information. The chief executive has hard information rather than hearsay on which to evaluate the performance of senior staff. The executive learns directly whether the delegatee can meet a deadline, can write well, and can learn on the job. The delegatees, by having had responsibility for a portion of the chief executive's portfolio, are groomed for advancement. As they tackle a variety of tasks, the chief executive learns where they are strong and where they need further improvement. One of them may emerge as the person to step in at least temporarily when you move on. When the time comes that a senior staff member is a candidate for a position elsewhere, you can give an authoritative and supportive recommendation.

Trust. Merely by delegating—thereby transferring some authority and responsibility—the chief executive expresses trust. As delegation succeeds, mutual trust grows.

General knowledge. Through delegation, knowledge is spread more widely and more people learn more about the organization. The culture of ideas—Senge's "learning organization" (1990)—is enabled and enhanced. When it is time to leave, you will have helped people to grow and you will leave an organization that is stronger at every level. Your legacy will be more apt to last.

Understanding why delegation is so valuable, next you need to learn how it is done.

How to Delegate

Delegation is an art. How to carry it out varies with the nature of the task and with the style, relationship, and experience of the chief executive and staff member. In contrast to Mark Twain (1923, p. 172), who said, "I do not like work even when another person does it," to make delegation effective you have to like and reward the good work of others.

Here are some general guidelines:

Do not give up easily on the search for a delegatee. For each task that arrives on the chief executive's desk, follow

Coolidge's advice and ask with determination, "Who else can do this?" If the answer is "Only I," be sure that answer is correct. You will be surprised by what others can do given the opportunity and the support. Do not delegate truly minor items; your assistant can handle them.

Delegate clearly. Make sure that your delegatees have both the responsibility for the task and the authority to carry it through. Make it clear that you are entrusting the task to the delegatee but that you will take ultimate responsibility for the product. Be prepared to give credit if it is successful; to take the blame if it is not (Jenks and Kelly, 1985).

Provide clear instructions. Describe the kind of product you expect to receive and when. If it is to be a written report, indicate how long it should be and whether you are the sole audience. Explain whether you intend to check on the progress of the task or to wait until the deadline. Let delegatees know that they can come to you for advice.

Hold the delegatee accountable and follow through. Subject the report to a high standard of review. If it is late, ask where it stands. If it is of inferior quality, send it back. You want your staff to know that when you delegate, you expect them to deliver a product of high quality on schedule.

Increase the level of responsibility. As your senior staff prove their ability to accept delegation, begin to give them more important and difficult assignments. Eventually, to see how well they handle it, give them one that you really should carry out yourself. Let them draft a report to the board, accompany you to make the request for a major gift, or represent the institution at an important meeting. By locating their strengths and weaknesses, you will be able to help them improve and advance in their careers.

Resist attempts at reverse delegation. Do not allow one of your senior staff to get you to take responsibility for actions and decisions that are rightfully theirs. Some such requests should be returned immediately with instructions; others can sometimes be ignored. After realizing that you are not going to take care of the matter, the staff member in question will often go ahead and do so.

In summary, the lesson of this section is: delegate, delegate, delegate. You and your organization both will benefit.

Using Information Technology

Using time efficiently, making meetings worthwhile, and delegating will make you and your organization more productive. The topic of this last section has even greater potential than these combined; it can transform the way an individual works and the way an entire organization functions. Unfortunately, with the exception of some universities and colleges, most nonprofits have not made effective use of information technology (Te'eni and Speltz, 1993). The obstacles are the expected ones: cost, lack of expertise and leadership, resistance to change. To overcome these barriers, the chief executive must endorse the importance of information technology, provide the funds, and, ideally, set an example.

What is the case for information technology? Although the first computer dates only to 1946 (the birth of ENIAC) and the first personal computer to the late 1970s, it is becoming clear that this new machine will prove at least as important an invention as the printing press. Some even predict that the information revolution will rank with the industrial revolution. Admittedly, early predictions of the way the computer would revolutionize education or provide productivity gains in industry have yet to be fully realized, and so far it has had little impact on the average home. Several recent studies, however, are showing that productivity gains have resulted from the use of information technology. Perhaps we have been impatient: it took two decades, for example, for American industry's investment in electrical motors to produce significant productivity increases.

However, it seems safe to predict that by the turn of the century, information technology will indeed have transformed how we work, learn, and live. An organization that fails to use information technology effectively is not only missing a current opportunity, it is incurring a deficit that will simply have to be made up later. In other words, nonprofits will soon lose the apparent option of deciding whether to use information technology: they will have to do so.

For the chief executive, information technology raises two key questions: (1) how can executives maintain budgetary and intellectual control over the area? and (2) how can executives benefit from information technology in their own administrative work? This section addresses the first issue; Resource E covers the second by providing a primer on how an executive can learn to use the computer. If you do not know how to use one of these machines, I urge you not to put off learning any longer. Not only will you then be able to obtain the direct benefits of using the computer, you will become more familiar with the lingo and less apt to be overwhelmed by the expertise of others.

Budgetary control is critical because information technology is costly: leading universities spend somewhere between 5 and 8 percent of their annual budget on it, which is as much as or more than they spend on their libraries (the distinction becomes moot as libraries are increasingly computerized). Other nonprofits will not need (or be able) to go that far, but information technology will take up an increasingly large slice of their budgetary pie. The chief executive cannot give up final authority over expenditures that not only are this large but that have such implications for the growth and development of the organization. At least a rudimentary understanding of computers and networking and their benefits is important and not difficult to obtain. After all, the chief executive is not expected to be an expert on many aspects of the mission and operation of the organization, so why make an exception in the case of information technology? Here is how to maintain the control that the chief executive must have:

- Make sure that the person in charge of information technology is knowledgeable and is someone in whom you have complete confidence. Beware the empire builder and the jargon user who wishes to confuse rather than enlighten. You might be better off to contract for your information technology services (see Chapter Six).

- Hire consultants periodically to review your institution's use of information technology and to provide you with an informed outside opinion. EDUCOM, a nonprofit consortium, provides excellent consultants.

- Learn as much as you can about the subject yourself.

Here is how one organization benefited from the use of information technology; other nonprofits are using such technology not only for electronic mail, word processing, and "spreadsheeting" but also for planning, project management, presentations, decision making, and brainstorming.

A new chief executive of an institution with two branches in one city observed that staff wasted a great deal of time traveling from one branch to the other for meetings and attempting to reach each other by telephone. Having come from an institution that used electronic mail extensively, she saw how to make her new organization much more productive. Obtaining a grant from a local foundation, she established a local area network in each of the two branches and persuaded a local university to allow each branch to connect to its Internet node. This allowed staff at one branch to send messages and files to staff at the other over the Internet. Travel time and "telephone tag" were sharply reduced; productivity rose.

Information technology is changing the world; make sure that it changes your organization.

5

Assembling Your Team

*Administrative subordinates either agree with the
president, change the president's mind, or resign.*
James L. Fisher, Power of the Presidency

The chief executive ultimately stands or falls on the quality of the senior staff. Therefore, although successful executives are always fair, they make needed personnel changes promptly. To put together a topflight team of senior administrators requires two connected actions: (1) evaluating your staff and discharging those whom you deem incapable of measuring up, and (2) filling vacancies, however created, with the best qualified persons you can find.

Evaluating and Replacing Senior Staff

Ultimately, how well your senior staff members perform and how well you work with them determines how you yourself are evaluated. The quality of your staff heavily influences your own future because you are responsible to the board for staff performance. The board is apt to accept only once, and then only in your first year, the excuse that one of your staff has let you down. Your job is to have staff who do not. This requires that you be fair and humane but resolute in your demand for excellence. Here are some suggestions for evaluating your senior staff:

- During the first few months, ask them to prepare a self-evaluation listing their accomplishments over the past year, their assessment of weaknesses and problems outstanding, and their objectives for the next year. This report will tell you the extent to which the senior staff member can complete an important task on schedule; understands his or her own strengths and weaknesses; can admit at least some of the latter; and can produce a realistic action agenda. This self-evaluation will provide a standard against which to measure performance in the future.

- Monitor your personal relations with each. Even though you are not to become the best of friends, a feeling of mutual respect and trust must exist.

- Make it clear that you welcome ideas and note how often each senior staff member brings one to you. Those who never do cannot help you to become an agent of change and may obstruct you.

- Determine whether the staff member follows through on your ideas and suggestions or whether in reality your agenda is being subverted or ignored in favor of the staff member's own.

- Give each member a difficult but achievable task and see how well he or she performs.

If it begins to appear that you may need to let a staff member go, approach the decision with great care. As Gilmore (1988) points out, an asymmetry exists: "If you remove someone you should not have, you may never learn of the contributions that the person might have made. If on the other hand . . . you [keep] someone you should not have, you learn directly by the person's failure" (p. 150). Thus, one should not rush to judgment. Gilmore balances this conservative (in the best sense of the word) position by reminding us, "A motivated person in the right role and an unmotivated person in the wrong role are several orders of magnitude apart in terms of the value they can add to an organization" (p. 160). If after a fair evaluation you firmly conclude that a particular staff member has not earned your confidence and must be replaced, you must steel yourself and do it.

When you lose confidence in someone, you rarely regain it. If you delay, you compromise the quality of your senior administration and thus the overall performance of the institution. In reviewing my own experience in replacing senior staff, I can find no examples in which I acted too quickly. Rather, when my timing was wrong, it was when, attempting to be fair, I waited too long. The longer you wait, the more damage can be done by rumors and the more likely it is that the person in question will learn about your plans through the grapevine and do harm or muster support. A person who is being let go should hear it from you, not through the rumor mill.

You will find it useful to consult several people confidentially: the chair of your board and a few other key members, your institutional lawyer, and where appropriate an outplacement consultant. Do not share your intention with more than a few board members, however, lest you lose confidentiality and appear to be asking the board to evaluate and choose your staff for you, a sure way to undermine your authority.

You need to share your intent with the board chair for several reasons. First, you want to be sure to follow the cardinal rule: no surprises. Second, the chair will have fired people and will have some useful advice for you. Third, you need to gain the support, or at least acquiescence, of the chair. If the staff member in question has been employed at the institution for several years, a base of support may have been built up with board members and you may need the chair to back your decision. If the chair is reluctant to support you, insist that as chief executive you must have the authority to choose your own team. Realize, however, that you are now on dangerous ground.

If the chair refuses, you either have to give up some of the authority of your office, and probably not for the last time, or consider resigning. (Of course, you should use all your skills to avoid putting yourself in a position where resignation becomes the only way out.) Thus, make sure that you have marshaled all your arguments. Ideally, the chair and the other board members with whom you consult will say, "Congratulations. I was waiting to see how long it would take you to recognize the deadwood and clear it out."

The sooner you let your institutional lawyer in on your intention the more help can be provided. You need to make sure that you have followed all the required steps, some of which are sure to limit your ability to dismiss a staff member without an extensive paper trail and justification. And no matter how poor the performance, it is increasingly likely these days that the person being dismissed will immediately consult a lawyer and at least threaten a lawsuit. You may have to engage in a complicated legal settlement and will need your lawyer's advice from the outset. Do not waste your time by thinking otherwise, or behave as did this executive:

> The chief executive of a professional organization, after letting his negative feelings build for several months and without consulting anyone, became fed up and fired a staff member on the spot, informing him that it was for poor performance. The staff member consulted an attorney, who discovered that none of the chief executive's complaints had been put in writing and that the fired staff member had in fact received positive evaluations and salary increases every year. In order to avoid a suit as well as having to reinstate the staff member, the organization had to provide two years' severance pay, outplacement, and extension of retirement benefits. The costs resulted in an organizational deficit and the chief executive appeared rash and imprudent.

For most people, nothing is worse to contemplate than having to fire someone. Some simply cannot do it; they should not become

chief executives. Dismissing a senior staff member is the most difficult part of the chief executive's job. (One manual on nonprofit
leadership included a chapter headed, "Can you fire your best
friend?" The answer surely should be no—avoid the painful necessity by never becoming best friends with one who reports to you.)
But once the decision has been made, if Macbeth's statement
" 'twere well it were done quickly" (*Macbeth*, 1.7.1) applies to anything, it is to firing a senior associate. As a protective device, perhaps, some executives have to work themselves into a state of anger
before they can do so. But this is too costly psychologically both for
you and for the person whom you are letting go. A professional does
not view that person as an enemy (even though he or she may turn
out to be one).

Here are some suggestions:

Do everything possible in advance so that an appropriate paper
trail justifies your action. Unfortunately, the new chief executive will not have had time to do so, and chances are that the
predecessor will have had a different view so that no record of
criticism exists. In that case, you may have to be prepared to
offer a more generous settlement than otherwise. But do not
let this forestall action.

Make an appointment to meet with the staff member late in the
day. Do not indicate the reason for the meeting.

Consider having a witness. An executive tells of becoming
frightened during a meeting at which she fired a male staff
member who appeared to be on the verge of violence. You too
may wish or need to have someone else present, if for no other
reason than to have a witness to substantiate your own
account of the meeting.

Do not discuss anything else in the meeting except your decision and come to the point immediately. Do not go into detail
as to why you are taking the action—the staff member will

likely be in a state of shock and unable to hear or to understand much of what you are saying. A long explanation merely provides the basis for further argument; the individual is not apt to agree in any case. Make it clear that your decision falls within your prerogative as chief executive, that you have consulted the board chair, and that it is final and irrevocable. You should never have to fire the same person twice.

Indicate when the action is to take effect and describe the settlement that you (and your counsel) propose. Then hand the staff person a written description of the settlement.

End the meeting and insist that the staff member take the rest of the day off.

This entire process should take no longer than fifteen minutes. The longer you allow it to go on, the more painful it is for everyone.

How to handle the actual departure date is difficult and varies from case to case. Most experts advise that the person should leave the premises at once and return only after-hours, under supervision if necessary, to clean out the office. Experience indicates that neither the institution nor the individual benefit from an extended period in which to close up shop and to say goodbye. In fact, the morale of both may decline. Experience also shows that some individuals who have been fired, even those who have seemed most loyal, are the first to turn on the institution and the chief executive. Their continued presence would be too destructive.

In cases where neither loyalty nor competence is in question and performance is not the issue—where the chief executive merely wants to have his or her own appointee in the position—it may be feasible to allow the individual to resign and to remain while seeking another position. But this is difficult to do well; few will be fooled into thinking that the resignation is voluntary. In any case, the world understands that a new chief executive wants his or her own team and little stigma is attached to a senior staff member dismissed early in the tenure of a new executive. People are as likely to assume that the executive is eccentric and wrong as that the departing staff member is incompetent.

Although common in the business world, outplacement services have not been used by most nonprofits, though some outplacement firms specialize in the sector. They could be used more often. Larger institutions have salaries that are high enough to justify the expense; smaller ones could band together to contract for such services. The argument for their use is that, although one chief executive may have to remove a few people in a career, a professional who specializes in outplacement will have assisted with the removal of hundreds. Their experience is invaluable; they can help you decide if you ought to do it and advise you on how to go about it.

A good outplacement consultant, like a good marriage counselor, will first meet with you to explore whether the relationship can be salvaged. If it cannot, the consultant will go over every detail of the settlement and coach you on how to handle the meeting at which you give the staff member the bad news. Often the consultant will be available nearby to meet with the individual immediately afterward.

Outplacement firms charge 15 to 20 percent of the salary of the person being let go. The expenditure is justified by the feeling that you have done all you could and by the increased support the board will provide knowing that the departing individual is being well taken care of. In return, the outplacement firm will provide an office with all the accoutrements, regular counseling, a secretary, and assistance with a résumé, allowing the departing individual to feel like a professional and to get a quick start on seeking another position.

Many nonprofits today are reducing staff size or downsizing, in which case employees are let go without any implication of poor performance. In those instances, the way can often be smoothed by having the organization provide some of the benefits of outplacement, such as the use of an office and secretary either on the premises or through an outside firm.

Whatever the cause of a staff member's departure, attention must be paid to the morale of the member's colleagues. Alleged details of any settlement usually get around, and are likely to be incorrect. Without revealing confidential information, the chief executive needs to be able to show other senior staff members that the departed colleague was treated at least as fairly as he or she deserved.

Painful as is the decision to remove a senior staff member, in many if not most cases the individual who is let go winds up in a more suitable position, one in which the likelihood of success is greater. You do no one a service by retaining a person who cannot perform to your standards. Requiring a fresh start elsewhere may be the greatest favor you can do the person who is departing. Seldom will it be seen that way, however, although here is an exception:

> The chief executive of a nonprofit reluctantly concluded that a vice president who had served for many years had run out of steam and had to be let go. His conclusion was well documented and he consulted with the board chair, an attorney, and an outplacement consultant. A fair settlement was offered and accepted. A year later, the departed staff member was running a thriving consulting business from his home. He wrote to say that the chief executive had been right after all, he had been burned out but now was happy and productive again.

Hiring New Staff

Assembling and maintaining the senior leadership team is the most important task facing the new chief executive. When a vacancy arises, for whatever reason, the first issue will be to determine whether the position is absolutely necessary or whether it can be merged with another in a reorganization. In these days of shrinking budgets, few positions can or should be automatically filled. The best time to make a change is when a senior position is vacant: you have one less response to consider.

As you have been evaluating staff and getting to know the organization, you will have been considering its structure and hierarchy. If you think a change in the organization chart may be in order, give it careful thought. Too often a new chief executive makes organizational changes quickly, partly to show that a new leader is in charge. This can be disruptive and embarrassing when after a few more months the now not-so-new chief executive has to change the organization again. Be patient and be sure that the changes you make in the organizational structure will last. As Gilmore (1988) notes, even the best reorganization consumes large amounts of the executive's most precious resource: time. Before you plunge ahead, make sure that you know enough about the organizational structure and the people themselves to be able to tell which is the greater source of difficulties.

In a well-run organization, every senior administrator, including the chief executive, should have someone who could step in at least temporarily should the administrator be absent for any reason. Before turning to the outside, look carefully at your existing staff to determine whether you have a person who could be promoted into the vacant position. Organizations should promote from within from time to time to build staff morale. Finding no serious contenders internally might indicate that the organization lacks depth in other areas as well.

The rest of this chapter is based on the assumption that after careful analysis you have decided to fill a senior-level opening from the outside (your organization may be required to have an external search, to which internal candidates can always apply). How you go about the search is critical not only in determining the quality of the person you hire but in setting the tone for your relationship with that person. Further, the way a search is conducted has an important bearing on the success of the appointee. Indeed, the search process should be thought of not in isolation but as an integral first phase of any new appointment. In this sense, the new appointment begins when the search starts, not when it ends.

Searches may go wrong in more ways than one. A poorly run

search will be apt to drive away the best candidates. An efficiently conducted search that nevertheless violates institutional norms may result in the appointment of a well-qualified candidate who is never viewed as legitimate and who never has a chance to succeed.

A great deal has been written about how searches should be conducted. The Association of Governing Boards, for example, has some useful publications. Chapter Two of this book describes how searches are conducted at the larger institutions, so this chapter will focus on the role of the chief executive in hiring senior staff.

Here are some points to keep in mind:

Internal candidates. Even though you have concluded otherwise, in all likelihood someone on your staff has been waiting for the position to open up, assuming that they will be promoted into it. Their disappointment if they are not to be considered may be reflected in their search for a position elsewhere, which is acceptable, or in grumpiness and poor performance, which is not. One of the initial duties of the new appointee will be to evaluate the staff, including this would-be heir apparent.

Search committee. Decide whether a formal search committee is necessary (or required). At a small institution, often it will not be. At a larger one, no formal committee would be required for, say, a search for a chief financial officer. But where the position has a wide constituency or institutional norms demand it—for example, the vice president of education at a museum or the deanship of a college—a search committee will be necessary. In such cases, set up the committee using the procedures that are accepted at the institution. In some instances, you can simply appoint the committee; in others, you will need to consult with one or more constituencies before doing so. At the smaller institutions, the committee may consist of the chief executive and a trustee or two.

Job description. After completing these steps and consulting as necessary, prepare a draft job description. If you are using a search committee, have the statement reviewed and endorsed by the committee.

Charge to committee. Search committees need to be given carefully developed charges so that they understand precisely what it is they being asked to do: whether to present one candidate or several; if several, whether they are to be ranked. For a senior position reporting to the chief executive, the committee should present an unranked list of acceptable candidates from whom you will select your preference. Otherwise, you may wind up selecting the third person on the committee's list, who happens to be your first choice but obviously not theirs. The word will quickly get around that you overruled the committee and that the appointee is not the most qualified. Insist that every name on the unranked list be truly acceptable to the committee.

Using a Search Consultant

Any chief executive who can afford to do so should consider using a search consultant. Here are the arguments in favor:

Experience. This first argument is identical to the case for using an outplacement consultant. In a career, one chief executive will hire several senior people, but search firms are involved in the hiring of hundreds or thousands. They have a depth of experience that far exceeds that which one chief executive could ever gain.

Information. In the early stages of the search, a good consultant will interview you, members of the search committee, and others. You will gain information about the position, about yourself, and about your organization that will not only help you refine the job description but will help the new appointee to be successful.

Communication. By asking the right questions of the search committee at the right time, a good consultant will keep the search process moving along in an orderly fashion. The consultant can deliver a message to the committee that would be awkward for you as the hiring chief executive to give, and vice versa.

Details. The search firm can handle all the clerical work and all the initial screening. In a search in which several score applications and nominations are received, this can relieve an enormous burden.

Some firms will take over the entire process and, while keeping you closely informed, ultimately give you the small number of finalists that you requested.

Equity. Although employed by the institution, search firms also feel an obligation both to the professions with which they work and to the advancement of individuals. They will attempt to make sure that the process is fair to all. After all, only one of the candidates will get the job; the search firm will wish to include some of the others in subsequent searches that it handles. You want candidates to be treated fairly and respectfully and searches to be conducted in such a way that your institution's reputation is enhanced.

Connections. Search consultants know of candidates from whom you otherwise would never hear. An experienced consultant will immediately be able to identify several who are qualified. The consultant can approach those individuals and others who might be interested, as well as those who have applied or been nominated, and approach them on a confidential, nonbinding basis. Besides the time required, it is more difficult for you as chief executive to make these overtures—you do not want to be in a position of appearing to entice someone to apply, ultimately only to reject that person, as you will with all but one of the candidates. Nor do you wish to become known for stealing the favorite employees of your chief executive colleagues. The consultant can stay in touch with promising but reluctant candidates over a period of months; you may not wish to do so lest you seem too interested.

Confidentiality. In the search consultant, several types of candidates and potential candidates have a source of confidential information: those who learn of the opening but who are not ready to apply or be nominated; those who do not want their current institution to learn that they would consider moving; those who simply need more information.

Mediation. Just as a real estate broker, labor mediator, or pair of divorce lawyers can put together an agreement that would fall apart if the two parties tried to negotiate face-to-face, so a good search consultant can act as an effective mediator in the final stages of negotiation. Both parties then have someone to whom they can turn knowing that their statements and demands need not prove final. Face can be saved; harder bargains can be struck. The consultant can indicate whether the candidate's requirements are in the correct range or tell the institution that it needs to offer a higher salary to avoid losing the candidate.

However, there are arguments against hiring a consultant. Search firms typically charge 30 percent of first year's salary plus expenses, though some specialized nonprofit consultants charge less and do a good job. Many nonprofits today do not have such funds readily available. (If the average appointee remains in the job for several years, however, the average yearly cost of having used a search firm is small.)

Also, although an appointment can often be traced directly to the efforts of a search consultant, just as often the appointee will have entered the search without the help of the consultant. (The difficulty is that one cannot know in advance which alternative a given search will produce. A certain amount of faith is required. And even where the consultant does not locate the successful candidate, all the other benefits of using a search consultant still pertain.)

Search firms come in varying sizes and with their own areas of specialization. The larger ones will only be interested in a search for the chief executive of a large institution, but smaller ones can assist with searches for other senior staff members. Most firms have a salary cutoff. As in other cases where strength would flow from numbers, professional associations could contract with a search firm, which would lower the salary cutoff as well as the fee in return for a guaranteed level of business.

If you decide to use a search consultant, ask colleagues at similar institutions about their experiences and check references. Invite several firms who seem most promising to make a presentation to you and other staff members; include trustees if appropriate. Be sure to determine the fee and how expenses will be charged, and obtain a list of their clients. Ascertain who will actually be the liaison with your search—some firms send their "first team" out for presentations but then assign someone less impressive to handle the account.

Building the Pool

In each search, the question of women and minority candidates should be taken up directly. Admittedly, this is a difficult subject—board members and others are apt to have differing views about affirmative action. My own, after having presided over many searches and participated in hundreds, starts with two premises: (1) All human beings should have an equal opportunity to make the most of their talents and to achieve their potential. No one should be denied such an opportunity because of race or sex. (2) Any society, and especially one founded with our American ideals and our history, needs to draw on the full abilities of each citizen. Women and minorities need to be in positions of responsibility because we need their talents.

It is critical that in each search a maximum effort be made to establish the broadest possible pool, including the maximum number of qualified candidates of both sexes and all races. Even at larger organizations that may have someone in the role of affirmative action officer, I believe that it remains the responsibility of the chief executive to see that searches are conducted in such a manner.

Once a broad pool has been established and allowance has been made for the bias that many women and minorities have faced and still face, then the best qualified person should be hired regardless of race or gender. Work to build the largest, strongest, most diverse pool; many problems will then disappear and the quality of appointees will improve.

If you think back over searches in which you have participated as employer or candidate, you will note that the person who was finally hired spent at most an hour or two with the prospective supervisor. Even in even the most careful search, it is difficult for either party to learn much about the other. On the basis of a few hours and a few telephone calls, life-changing decisions are made. Thus, I have learned to follow the advice of Brian O'Connell (1993): "Do almost anything to find candidates who have already demonstrated a capacity to succeed." (p. 171). Nothing succeeds like success and Experience is the best teacher—these have become clichés because they are true. Look for an actual record of past accomplishments in a similar job or one that requires similar skills; this is the best predictor of future accomplishments.

Role of the Chief Executive

It is in the "end game" of the search process, where the effective decision is made, that the chief executive needs to be sure to get directly involved. When the executive enters the process depends on many factors but especially on whether a formal search committee is being used and, if so, the charge that was given to them. The more authority that has been delegated to such a committee, the more obtrusive the entry of the chief executive is apt to be. But at some appropriate time, you must become a direct participant in the appointment of the person who will report to you. Remember that a search committee and a consultant will not be around to take the blame should the appointment not work out. You will be, and you must have the major voice in the selection. After all, you know better than anyone the kind of person you seek, and therefore your opinion matters most. You will have to work closely with the appointee; only you can judge how good is the all-important chemistry between you.

However, maintaining influence over the search committee may be a delicate task. Sometimes it will be clear that you need consult only minimally. In other cases, you will need to persuade. Your task will be much easier if it has been made clear what procedures will be followed and if it is clearly understood by all from the outset that the chief executive has the final authority to make the appointment.

If a formal committee exists, review the dossiers of the finalists that the committee has developed and identify those who you feel should be invited for interviews. Here you are better off taking the positive stance of identifying potential winners than crossing off losers (some of whom are apt to be the favorite of someone else involved in the search process). An experienced search consultant will know you, the institution, and the list of candidates and can provide advice on the best fit. Through whatever process is used, the list will be pared down to a small group of interviewees. You will meet with these candidates and follow through to the end of the process. Here are the ground rules that you need to observe:

Meet with each finalist. You can meet for perhaps an hour early in the visit and again at the end. Get quickly beyond the small talk and on to questions whose answers will help you to choose. These are some of the most important conversations you will have; use them to maximum advantage.

Study the candidate's résumé. Study it before the initial meeting and do not ask questions that are clearly covered in it.

Ask specific questions. Of course, you may ask generic questions if you wish, such as, "What do you hope to be doing in ten years?" and "What are your strengths and weaknesses?" (see Resource A) but realize that an intelligent candidate will have prepared for them and that the answers to such questions will not help much in the final selection. You will learn much more if you have created a set of questions that probe the special qualities that are needed. You need only spend a half hour to come up with a much better list than if you make them up as the conversation proceeds. Remember that this is the first time that the candidate has met you and that both of you will form lasting impressions from the encounter. Take written notes on these conversations immediately; otherwise, they will be difficult to reconstruct.

Do not read from a prepared set of questions. Junior search consultants or inexperienced members of a search committee conducting a phone interview often read from a set of routine, generic questions that never lead to others but apparently are merely being checked off a list.

Ask whether the candidate has any questions. These can tell you whether the candidate had the interest and foresight to do the requisite homework and can reveal the candidate's ability to identify the important issues.

Try to gauge the depth of the candidate's interest. Ask whether there are special compensation or personal requirements with which you might help if the candidate gets the job. Try to make it clear that if an offer comes it will be because the candidate is your personal choice (as well as that of the search committee, if any.)

Once the on-site interviews are completed, you will be down to a very short list of finalists, perhaps only one person. How you proceed depends on how many there are and where they are located; here are some guidelines:

1. If the position is of critical importance, such as a chief financial or chief development officer, do not make an offer without spending an hour or two alone with the candidate, perhaps over a meal, and letting the candidate do most of the talking. Make it clear that the questions are over and that you now wish to get to know the candidate socially. Find out how comfortable you are together; if hired, you will spend much time together. If you are not comfortable, others may not be either.

2. Either the chief executive or the search consultant should speak directly with several of the references listed by the candidate. You should expect that these evaluations will be positive. They are necessary but not sufficient.

3. By the time you are ready to extend an offer—and you should do so personally—it should be assumed that the period of confidentiality is over. Now you should speak with the candidate's current supervisor. In addition, speak to two or three others who were not listed as references. In these conversations, ask questions that a professional must answer honestly and that will give you information that may not have come out before. Ask such questions as these: What are the candidate's strengths and weaknesses as you have personally observed them? Knowing what you know about me and my institution, would you hire this candidate? Is there anything about the candidate that I ought to know that I might not have already learned? If I hire the candidate, what skills would need strengthening? Is there anything else you want to tell me? You might not ask all of these questions of any one reference or ask them in exactly this way. But rather than trying to find precisely the right question to ask references, you must assume that they are honest and that their professional standards and reputation are more important to them than whether a given candidate, even a close protégé, gets a given job. You want to force a shift in loyalty away from the candidate and toward—if not you personally—then at least a sense of personal professionalism. In other words, structure the conversation within the boundaries of veracity and professionalism and you will learn what you need to know.

4. Consider a visit. Some nonprofit chief executives visit the home organization of their final choice or two. This helps them to better to understand the candidate by having seen the context in which he or she has worked and been successful. The candidate is impressed that a busy chief executive has gone to such lengths. This step may place the unsuccessful candidate at risk, however, and needs to be thought through carefully.

Letters of Reference

Thousands of letters of recommendation cross the country daily, yet seldom does one make a substantial difference in a search. When was the last time that you read a letter of recommendation that contained any substantial criticism? After all, only those who will write a positive letter are asked for one. Further, today an organization is often required by law to allow staff members to have access to their files. Since one may have to go on working with that person, criticism is tempered. (One college was required to open the files of all faculty hired over a seven-year period, files that included many letters written in the belief that they would be held confidential. This act was perpetrated by the Equal Employment Opportunity Commission [EEOC] in response to a claim by a rejected professor of French that he had been denied tenure because he was of foreign birth. His native land? France.)

Taken together, these developments mean that only an enemy would write an honestly negative letter of recommendation; as noted, they are not asked. The adulterated letters that do result are at best uninformative and at worst seriously misleading. Instead, pick up the telephone and call—one telephone call, if handled correctly, can be worth any number of letters of recommendation.

Final Negotiations

Eventually, the search process will have produced a single candidate whom you wish to hire. You may have a chance to make the offer during a visit to the candidate's home institution; if not, it is apt to be made over the telephone. If you have followed good practice, by this time you will know about how much compensation will have to be offered and whether the candidate is likely to accept. You should also have established that your policy is to offer more than the candidate's current salary, yet you must be constrained by the salary schedule of your institution. Determine how close to the top of your range the candidate should earn, and then call and make that offer, explaining how you arrived at it and that it is the highest salary you can extend and still be fair to the institution. In almost every case, a candidate who really wants the job will accept an offer described in this way. Now and again, however, one will ask for more. Do not agree without receiving a clear and persuasive explanation, one that perhaps reveals an aspect of the candidate's finances of which you had been unaware. If you receive such a clarification, to show that you heard the candidate's argument and that you truly want an acceptance, be prepared to move to a slightly higher offer. If that does not produce agreement, immediately break off the negotiations, cross that candidate off your list, and move on to your next choice. A chief executive should not be placed in the undignified position of appearing to haggle over hundreds of dollars. Furthermore, you do not want to hire a senior associate who may have taken the job mainly for financial reasons, who may annually subject you to this kind of unpleasant haggling, and who either does not respect institutional norms or does not believe what you have said about them. Here is an example of the process gone wrong:

> After a lengthy search, a chief executive made a salary offer to a candidate who had interviewed well and whose letters of reference were positive. The candidate said that she needed time to consider. The next day, the candidate came back with an account of her particular difficulties, which included a recalcitrant former spouse and mortgage payments on a house that would be difficult to sell. The chief executive agreed to increase the salary offer. The candidate called again to say that a more careful review of benefits showed that the move would cost the equivalent of $750 annually and asked for this to be made up in salary. The chief executive again agreed. Finally, the candidate called to ask for assistance with moving expenses, which had been explicitly ruled out during the search; she stated that this was the only obstacle now remaining. The chief executive buckled again, agreeing to pay half of moving costs, and the deal was finally struck. Once on the job, this candidate was seldom satisfied with her salary, her benefits, the location and decor of her office, and her required attendance at important staff meetings. She proved to be a constant thorn in the side of this weak chief executive.

Postacceptance

If the position is currently vacant, the new appointee should resign and join you soon. Most will overestimate how long they need to stay. For a person who is at or moving into a senior staff position, a month is long enough. The old institution will be better off with an early departure, you with an early arrival.

Once an acceptance has been received, most institutions return to business as usual. You can do better. Invite your new colleague (and spouse if there is one) to come for a visit and begin to send information about the institution. If the appointee comes from out of town, assign a staff member to assist with housing, schools, and the like. Establish a strong link immediately and drive home the notion that he or she is now a member of your team at your institution. Once the appointee arrives on the job, arrange a series of lunches or dinners and begin to make introductions to key individuals: trustees, donors, friends of the institution.

With your senior team assembled, you are now ready to proceed to master the essential tools of administration: budgeting, planning, and evaluation.

. . . .

6

Mastering the Budget

A fool and his money are soon parted.

English proverb

Nonprofits exist to fulfill a mission, corporations to reward their stockholder-owners. Perhaps the principal difference is that a nonprofit cannot return a surplus to the owners: even if there is a surplus, there are no owners. However, both kinds of organization must earn a "profit" in the sense that over the long run revenues must exceed expenses. A vital task for the nonprofit chief executive, and in the eyes of the board often the most important task, is to produce and to maintain financial stability. Beyond the fiscal prudence and good management necessary to break even, organizations need to have enough funds to support new ideas—what we might call "internal venture capital." Without that, change will be retarded. Few nonprofits today have such funds; all should be striving to obtain them.

Financial Management and Planning

A nonprofit chief executive can spend so much time raising money and overseeing the budget that not enough is left for other leadership responsibilities. Important as it is, finance remains a means and not an end. For the sake of the future of the organization, while ensuring responsible financial oversight, the chief executive simply must free up time to think, to plan, and to lead. Therefore, the chief executive needs the services of first-class chief development and chief financial officers (read controller, treasurer, vice president for finance, finance director) to whom the routine matters can be delegated, saving the chief executive's time for leadership activities. Many smaller nonprofits will not be able to have either a finance director or a development director, but all should aspire to.

To be successful at raising funds, you have to be able to demonstrate that you are managing responsibly those you already have; therefore, financial management is especially critical. The new chief executive should evaluate the financial officer and if not satisfied move immediately to find a replacement. Certainly the first full budget year should not be entered without a chief financial officer in whom you have complete confidence.

The new chief executive should review the financial statements from the preceding five years. (If you do not understand the rudiments of fund accounting or how to read a balance sheet, you might ask a mentor for help or take one of the short seminars given by many banks, accounting firms, and professional societies. Given the proclivity of the bodies that determine accounting rules to revise and add, even experienced chief executives may benefit from retooling.) With the help of the chief financial officer, distinguish between the published surplus or deficit and the "real" one. Many institutions include in their public operating statements transfers, investment gains, accruals, and other income that have little or no bearing on the strength of their core operations. They appear to have run a "profit" but in fact did not. Look to see whether the core operations of the organization are supported by dependable revenue sources. Look also for departments that chronically exceed their budget, that have odd year-end spending patterns, or that seem to receive unusual favors. If you find them, ask the chief financial officer why procedures were not in place to prevent such practices. In the following example, a well-meaning executive overdid it:

A small art institute that fell into financial difficulty fired its director and hired another. After the second budget year of the new appointment, the director announced that the institute had run a surplus for the first time in a decade. A similar announcement was made during each of the next three years. The institute was then visited by accreditors, who discovered that the surpluses existed only "below the line"; that is, the core operations had continued to run deficits, which had been offset by nonmandatory transfers from endowment and other funds. These transfers had been duly noted in financial reports but they and the director's rhetoric had been accepted by the trustees in the interest of establishing a positive image for the institute.

Especially at the beginning of your appointment, do not be afraid to ask the "dumb question." Your financial officer knows that you are were not hired because of your financial acumen. If you fail to ask a question when first confronted with the need, it will often prove embarrassing to raise it later and you will forgo the chance, only to be more embarrassed when a trustee asks you the same "dumb question" and discovers that you do not know the answer.

Ask the chief financial officer to provide a five-year financial forecast using a spreadsheet model. Every organization, no matter how small or poorly equipped, must somehow be able to use spreadsheets, the single most useful management tool since the adding machine. A well-done financial forecast requires several steps that are useful in themselves:

1. All critical financial variables must be identified.
2. Their current levels must be specified.
3. Reasonable assumptions must be made about their rates of growth.

Review this forecast with the chief financial officer and then with your senior staff. Discussing which variables are truly critical, making sure that you know their current levels, and debating whether the assumptions used are truly reasonable is a valuable exercise. To avoid "groupthink," rotate the role of devil's advocate, the person who asks tough questions about each assumption.

The first forecast may well show a rosy future: increasing surpluses over the entire five-year period. Go back and reexamine the assumptions, remembering that revenue tends to be overestimated and expenses tend to be underestimated. Even if the assumptions seem reasonable, beware: few nonprofits run increasingly large surpluses year after year. To do so simply is not consonant with their financing and with their mission of service. Nonprofits need to make a modest "profit," but they are not set up to handle large ones. A private college that recorded large surpluses would soon find a revolt among tuition-paying parents; a public one would soon find its legislative appropriations cut. Arts and social service agencies in most cases do not even have the option of running a substantial surplus. All nonprofits should remember that funders want to see fiscal health but not wealth. Thus, if through good luck or good management a nonprofit should find itself with growing surpluses, it would either lower its income by charging less or increase its expenditures by creating worthwhile new programs. It would not run larger and larger surpluses.

Annual Budgeting

The five-year forecast should be used as the starting point for preparation of the annual budget. Many books and manuals have been written about budgeting; the intent of this chapter is not to describe the entire process but to outline the role of the chief executive in it. Ideally, even at the smaller institutions, the executive will delegate the details of annual budgeting to the chief financial officer. Use the bully pulpit to explain to your senior staff why the budget must be balanced at the beginning and at the end of each year and that you have invested the chief financial officer with the authority to see that it does.

All but a fortunate few nonprofits have uncertainty inherent in their budget planning and execution, and many are vulnerable. Museums and zoos, which depend on the public buying a ticket in certain numbers, can be severely affected by the weather and by economic conditions. Institutions that depend on state or municipal funding can suddenly find their appropriation cut. All institutions are subject to ups and downs in gifts and grants from private and government sources; the smaller nonprofits are often extremely vulnerable. Most colleges and universities, with the exception of the highly selective, must scramble to fill their enrollment targets and often cannot know whether they have met them until the academic year has begun, too late to correct. Even well-endowed research universities are at risk, as we learned when the federal government reduced the indirect cost allowance recovery rate.

Despite these vulnerabilities, the chief executive is expected to balance the budget. Since much of the final result is controlled by external forces that can at best only be influenced, how can you be certain that the budget will be in balance? One key is that few organizations begin the year planning to run a deficit. Almost all start with a budget that is either balanced or that shows a modest surplus. These budgets are prepared over several months, reviewed by trustees, and appear sound, but somehow when the year is over there is nonetheless a deficit.

Deficits show up due to faulty estimates, to faulty execution, or to both. Organizations tend to generate revenue estimates that are unrealistically high; otherwise, painful action such as laying off employees may be necessary. Often overly optimistic targets for fundraising become the final budget balancer. For similar reasons, expenditure estimates tend to be set too low. And poor management can result in neither estimate being achieved.

Planning and execution, however, are entirely within the control of the organization. They require a rigorous budget process and discipline:

Budget only those revenue increases that are supported by a thorough analysis and that are within historical trends. In organizations that cannot be certain that next year's revenue will be higher than this year's, which includes most nonprofits, the new chief executive would be well advised to budget no more revenue than actually received in the previous year and perhaps less. This is apt to require cuts in the expense budget.

Make the budget revenue driven. That is, develop a conservative revenue budget and then force the expense budget to conform to it. Instead of being allowed to present an unrealistic "wish list," departments will be told how much they have to spend.

Examine the targets and the results for your fundraising program. You may find that goals were unrealistically high, that execution was poor, or both. Set a target that stretches the performance of the fundraisers, but not to the breaking point.

Make sure that your chief financial officer has certified to you personally that all revenue and expenditure estimates in the budget are realistic. Chief financial officers tend to be conservative; one who says that the budget is acceptable, and whose job is on the line, can be believed.

If your organization receives program grants from funders, make sure that you are taking all the overhead allowed and that all salaries or fractions of salaries that can be legitimately paid by grants have been so charged.

When these steps have been taken, you will be in the best possible position to balance the budget.

Budget Ploys

The Effective Nonprofit Executive Handbook (Public Management Institute, 1980) contains a wealth of good ideas. Among the more

useful is its amusing but all-too-true analysis of the devices and stratagems used by clever staff members to obtain the results that they
want for their department in the annual budget process (p. 418).
Following are the stratagems (slightly rephrased):

Foot in the door	An initial budget known to be low will be raised later.
Hidden ball	Popular items are padded to support less popular ones.
Divide and conquer	"Mom, Dad didn't say no": senior staff are asked until one agrees.
Shell game	Source of program funds is obscured in category "other."
It's free!	Full costs are not revealed.
You are to blame	Supervisors said to be late in providing budget instructions.
We must be up-to-date	Latest technological advance is alleged to be essential.
Razzle-dazzle	Elaborate analysis proves the need.
Delayed buck	New procedures prevent budget submission until too late to change.
Sprinkling	Small, hard-to-detect percentage increases are spread throughout.
Make a study	Budget cannot be cut until more data available.
Gold watch	Only the budget for pens and paper clips can be cut.
We are the experts	Others lack the knowledge to question intelligently.
It will save staff	Costly new technology will pay for itself through staff reductions.

I only work here   Rules do not allow the requested change
                     in the budget.

Contingency Budget

Even if all the recommended steps have been taken and at the beginning of the year the budget is the best possible, unforeseen circumstances will develop. The way to protect against them, and indeed against the whole set of budgetary mishaps, is to have a large enough contingency line in the annual budget and to protect it ruthlessly. Set a target for the contingency budget that initially seems unreasonably high and try to reach it over several years.

Your review with the chief financial officer of past budgets will have given you a good idea of how vulnerable the organization has been and is. If you learn that deficits typically have run in the 5 percent range, you will need a contingency line at least that large. Larger is better here.

In order to find the funds to provide such a large contingency, reductions may be required, including cuts in staff size. But if you can effectively guarantee that the organization will not run further deficits, staff reductions may be worth the cost. Your appeal to outside funders and to your board then will be much stronger. Internally, you will be able to promise that, barring catastrophe, any further staff reductions will come through attrition, a promise that should help to raise staff morale. Here is a good example of the value of having a contingency line in the budget:

A metropolitan zoo had balanced its budget and achieved a contingency amounting to 8 percent. During the spring, its region was hit hard by a major hurricane, which did severe damage although almost all animals were saved. The zoo was unable to return to its prehurricane status for three months. The zoo used $75,000 of its contingency funds for an advertising blitz to announce that it was reopening and that the first day's admission would be free. The community responded with the highest annual attendance in the zoo's history.

> The zoo ended the difficult year with another balanced budget,
> though not the one that had been planned at the beginning.

Your goal is to have a balanced budget or modest surplus. Therefore, if after the midpoint of the fiscal year you are comfortable that
the budget will come in close to what is planned, you can judi-
ciously begin to spend the contingency on important items that did
not fit into the regular budget or that have arisen since it was prepared. For example, if one of your senior staff comes to you midway
through the fiscal year with a new idea requiring seed money, you
may be able to provide it.

You will also be well advised to try to include a provision for
reserves. These are larger than an annual contingency. O'Connell
(1993) recommends that they equal at least half of one year's operating expenses and are designed to help the organization survive a
true catastrophe, to ease cash flow problems, and even to provide
the venture capital that all organizations need. To develop such
reserves will be a tall order for most nonprofits, but it is a worthy
goal to try to achieve over time.

Controlling Expenditures

A critical part of financial management is to exercise firm control
once the year has begun, yet most nonprofits have difficulty doing
so. They may generate large amounts of budgetary information that
tells them, for example, which departments are overspending and
which have strangely erratic spending patterns, but they do too little with the information. Here are some tested suggestions:

Start the year with a revenue-driven, conservative budget, as
described above, and the largest contingency line that you can
generate.

Insist that no positions can be added to the budget and filled
outside the regular budget process. This allows for administrative control and the proper accounting of grant funds. Since

most nonprofits are labor intensive, controlling the size of staff and the source of their compensation is critical.

Personally authorize the filling of each vacancy and sign each letter of appointment (unless your organization is quite large). Make it known that without such a signed letter, employment is not official and staff cannot be paid. The chief executives of smaller organizations sign each check—that is the ultimate way to learn where the money goes.

Meet with the senior staff at the start of the fiscal year and tell them clearly that running a deficit is simply not an option. Remind them that all participated in the preparation of the budget and that it is everyone's responsibility to see that it is followed. You and the chief financial officer will provide them with all the support and information necessary, but they are accountable. The message is: if you cannot manage your budget, I will not be able to manage a salary increase, and eventually a job, for you.

From the first month of the fiscal year, have the chief financial officer meet monthly with each department head to go over the results to date and to spot trouble ahead. These managers will in turn meet with those who report to them, conveying the same information. Ignorance of budgetary facts will not be an acceptable excuse. The chief financial officer will also report to the chief executive monthly on how the budget is progressing.

Have the chief financial officer reclaim all available monies and place them in the contingency budget. Funds not spent because of a delay in filling a vacancy will not remain with that department; they belong to the organization.

Sometimes, in spite of all of these measures, and even a sizable contingency, the chief financial officer and chief executive can see that the organization is heading for a deficit. This conclusion must, of course, be reached early enough for corrective action to be taken. If more severe steps are then judged to be necessary, include these:

Require written approval by the chief financial officer of each expenditure above a certain relatively modest level.

Freeze staff size; that is, allow no positions to be added and no vacancies to be filled automatically. Each time a vacancy occurs, require that an application for a replacement be made and weighed against other outstanding personnel and budgetary needs. If the need is great and the funds can be made available, the position may be filled. This technique means that staff size cannot grow and may shrink. (Many nonprofits have had to use this approach for years.)

Reduce staff if this step does not reduce expenditures sufficiently. Take advantage of attrition: prohibit all new hires and require that each time a vacancy arises for whatever reason, a replacement can come only through an internal transfer. Each such transfer opens another vacancy, which can be filled only by another internal transfer, and so forth, until a vacancy is reached that is of sufficiently low priority that it need not be replaced. Thus, each time a vacancy arises, staff size will necessarily be reduced by one. To make this process work, positions will have to be ranked in order of expendability, a step that may lower morale. But at this stage, that may be better than the alternatives.

If in spite of these techniques a balanced budget still cannot be assured, the organization's budget is seriously out of balance: its core revenues cannot support its core operations. A major, wholesale reorganization is required, with staff layoffs and possibly even a redefinition of mission and goals. Doing so will require a sound strategic plan.

Salary Administration and Performance

Almost without exception, the major expense item for any non-profit organization is staff compensation. Further, the procedures by which salary increases are determined and communicated critically affect staff morale. Most organizations conduct annual performance evaluations and many award differential, or merit, salary increases based on those evaluations. This process, which consumes massive amounts of time, money, and mental energy, typically is based on the following assumptions: that performance is distributed along the familiar bell-shaped curve; that performance can be measured with sufficient accuracy so as to place individual workers along that curve; that if workers are informed through salary increases where their performance is judged to lie along the curve, they will feel that they have been treated fairly and their morale and performance will improve.

Unfortunately, there is considerable evidence that each assumption is wrong. First, performance within a mature organization should not lie along a bell-shaped curve. Organizations screen their new hires carefully—they do not select them randomly—and they provide on-the-job training as well as various other performance improvement opportunities. Most employees work out satisfactorily, performing at or above the level expected. Where that is not the case, the employee either is counseled to a lower-level job or is fired. Instead of the familiar bell-shaped curve, therefore, actual performance lies along a curve that is highly skewed in the direction of superior accomplishment. Like the children of Garrison Keillor's Lake Wobegon, when compared to a theoretical distribution based on a random selection, the performance of most workers is above average.

Professionals know intuitively that this is true: it is not merely unfounded pride that causes over 90 percent of them, when surveyed, to rank their performance as above average. They implicitly recognize that the bell-shaped curve does not apply: that "average" is at least a complicated if not a meaningless concept with a curve so highly skewed. Evaluating such employees according to a bell-shaped curve is to wind up disappointing most of them.

Most organizations describe their salary increase systems in ways that make a bad situation worse. Officials tell employees that the system is accurate, fair, and careful, and they say, explicitly or implicitly, that it will lead to better performance and morale. When these benefits rarely turn out to be true, employees can draw one of two conclusions: senior management is boneheaded or is unable to tell the truth. When the same poor results occur year after year, boneheadedness no longer seems a possible explanation.

If all this were not bad enough, three other aspects of organizational behavior make it worse. First, most organizations use performance evaluation schemes that are overly complicated or that expect human beings to do things that they cannot or will not do, such as directly and repeatedly criticize those with whom they have to work daily. Second, these schemes often are poorly explained and difficult to understand. Third, sensing that their system is not producing improvements in morale and performance, many organizations—in a vain quest to improve matters—change the system frequently, sometimes, it seems, every year. This adds further confusion and makes equity harder to achieve.

Of course performance does vary, though not along a bell-shaped curve, and of course it can be assessed, though not as rigorously as we have pretended. Certainly it can be improved. The best systems will rely on the carrot rather than the stick and emphasize what people are doing right rather than what they are doing wrong.

A technique that some have found useful is the "90–10" system. The logic behind it is that, although well over half believe their performance to be above average, few truly believe that they belong in the top 10 percent. On the other hand, most believe that they know who does belong in the top 10 percent and would be willing to see those deserving individuals receive a higher increase, at least if it does not appear to come at their own expense. Identifying the top 10 percent does not require an elaborate process of evaluation and competition: talk with senior staff or conduct a survey of all employees, asking them to nominate their "top 10." This can be done in a way that rewards top performance and encourages everyone, and it may even improve morale.

In preparing the annual budget, set aside an amount for the salary pool that will allow the following actions:

- To the approximately 90 percent, award an across-the-board raise that if possible is above inflation. (To double standard of living over a thirty-five-year career requires annual increases that average 2 percent above inflation.)

- To the truly poor performers, give no increase and inform them that unless they have improved by the next evaluation, they may lose their jobs.

- To the top 10 percent, award an increase several percentage points above inflation. You might hold a ceremony in which they are publicly identified and thanked.

Performance evaluation and counseling, which can now be conducted separately from the salary review, can emphasize professional development. Employees can be told how their performance would need to improve for them to move into the top 10 percent.

One caveat is necessary: some of the same employees will tend to show up in the top 10 percent each year. If they were to receive annual salary increases well above the rest, eventually their salaries would grow out of line. Therefore, the system needs to be modified—for example, by using a rule that one who is in the top 10 two years in a row is ineligible for one or two subsequent years. These individuals would receive the across-the-board increase but would not be eligible for the larger increase.

A wide assortment of nonsalary rewards could be offered to outstanding performers: noncash prizes and awards; time off; recognition banquets; bonuses; stipends for special projects; cost of attending workshops and professional meetings; travel allowances. Lynch (1993) lists many possibilities and offers wise counsel on how such nonsalary rewards can be presented. His first of ten rules is "Give recognition or else" (p. 27).

The catch to all of this is, of course, that to award salary increases the organization must generate the money by increasing revenue or reducing expenses, perhaps through staff reductions. Most nonprofit chief executives sooner or later must decide whether to have more staff and pay them less, or vice versa. This is a key strategic decision that needs to be addressed in planning.

"Sell the Mail Room"

This phrase from Peter Drucker (1986) points up the importance and desirability of what has become known as "outsourcing": hiring specialty firms to perform certain tasks that fall outside the expertise and mission of the organization. Drucker argues that, since the mail room is the Siberia of organizations, if it is managed internally it will always perform poorly and at greater cost than necessary. No one truly wants to work there, no route upward in the organization exists, management cannot readily measure its cost-effectiveness. On the other hand, if one bids a contract for the mail room (that is, cleaning, parking, food service, stores, and even computing and financial services) to outside firms that specialize in operating mail rooms, one can take advantage of the competition and its expertise. Within such a firm, an entry-level employee can aspire to the presidency of the company. While retaining those direct, mission-related functions that cannot be bought at any price, nonprofits should consider outsourcing all routine services that they cannot do better than an outside firm. Here is an example:

> A large aquarium operated its own janitorial service. Turnover among janitorial employees was excessive, as were sick days; morale and performance were low. No member of the janitorial staff had ever been promoted to another position outside the department. Finally the aquarium decided to obtain bids from outside contractors. The president of the company with the lowest bid—25 percent lower than the cost of the institution's own janitorial services—had started as a janitor with the company. The bid was accepted and a three-year contract signed; performance and morale improved immediately. The contractor used total quality management techniques in a continual search for higher performance; poor performers were replaced before aquarium officials had a chance to complain.

With the budget under control, you are ready to look further ahead and to determine what ends your financial means can best serve.

7

Planning for Change and Quality

Plans are useless, but planning is indispensable.
Dwight D. Eisenhower

In *Leadership and Ambiguity,* Cohen and March (1986) note that although the presidents whom they interviewed in the early 1970s stressed the importance of broad institutional planning, none could point to a comprehensive plan for their institution. Could it be that, as with the weather, everybody talks about planning, but nobody does anything about it? At the time Cohen and March wrote, the answer was largely yes—planning was more praised than implemented. Today, many nonprofits have been or are engaged in planning; nearly all are aware that they should. Funders and trustees are beginning to insist, and that is all to the good.

As Ike's aphorism implies, however, a written plan is less important than continual engagement in the planning process. A plan can be put on the shelf and forgotten or followed blindly without regard to changes in basic assumptions. The process of planning, however, keeps the organization poised to take advantage of trends, to ward off threats, to flex and adjust as the times and changed conditions demand. This is advantageous, for the external conditions under which an organization operates seldom remain constant for long or turn out exactly as predicted.

In 1960, a major foundation asked selected institutions to outline their assumptions regarding developments that were likely during the next decade. Understandably, none foresaw the civil rights movement, the Viet Nam War, the protest generation, and stagflation. Had they been engaged in a process of planning, which few if any were in a formal way, they still could not have foretold the future, but surely they could have reacted more effectively when it arrived.

Planning is a formalized mechanism for inducing change. It reveals which changes will be made and when. No process is more important to the change agent than planning; therefore, the chief executive must promote, support, and lead it. Sometimes, planning will be comprehensive, reaching all parts of the organization. At other times, it will be more strategic, pointing to the solution of particular problems or the seizing of special opportunities. All planning should proceed concomitantly with sophisticated financial planning and ask similar questions:

- What data do we need?

- Do we have those data? If not, how and when are we to obtain them?

- For which factors do we need to make assumptions, and what are reasonable assumptions?

These are the starting points of a sound planning process.

The Great Questions

As a young student, one is asked to find the right answers. As education and then careers advance, and as maturity is gained, the "right answer" becomes an increasingly useless concept. Sometimes there is more than one answer; sometimes the answer that appears correct today turns out to be wrong tomorrow. Many important questions are so complex that the concept of a single right answer has no meaning. To make matters more difficult, the attempt to answer one question frequently raises others. In the long run, rather than the finding of the right answers, critical to the advancement of disciplines and organizations is the identification and the persistent raising of the right questions. In the sense that the examined life is the best attainable, this may also be true for individuals.

In nonprofit organizations, many important questions can and should be raised by senior staff, trustees, faculty, students, and others. They are most apt to feel free to do so if the organization embraces ideas and prizes questions, even those that may challenge some of its most fundamental beliefs and assumptions. But a set exists that we might call the great questions: those whose answers can determine the organization's future and even its survival. All organizations, from the largest to the smallest, have potentially great questions and need to seek them out. Failure to do so can have dire, even fatal, organizational consequences, as numerous examples from the corporate world over the last decade or two demonstrate. Often the chief executive will be the only person who has both the breadth of perspective to comprehend these questions and the authority and confidence to ask them. Taking the long view, ensuring that such questions are raised may indeed be the chief executive's most important opportunity and responsibility. Planning is critical because it provides an opportunity and a format in which the chief executive can ensure that the great institutional questions are asked.

The Planning Process

Planning is grounded in the mission, defines goals and the strategies for reaching those goals, and is based on information and measurement (Bryson, 1988). It maps the route by which change will occur. The process has many distinct benefits, some of which would not be found in its absence, others of which might be but not dependably so. As O'Connell puts it, "In the absence of more realistic planning, most voluntary agencies are governed, and badly so, by the *bright idea*" (1993, p. 79).

Most planning today is said to be strategic rather than long range. As the name suggests, strategic planning is aimed at identifying specific issues and finding strategies for resolving them. It focuses on a variety of possible futures and actions that can be taken in response, rather than on a description of the most likely future. Strategic planning is the connection between the mission and what people do day-to-day (Lynch, 1993) and accomplishes the following objectives:

- It forces long-range thinking, which otherwise tends to be driven out by the press of day-to-day duties.

- It illuminates the external conditions under which the organization will operate.

- It requires that the strategic issues—the fundamental problems to be solved or opportunities to be grasped—be identified, that they be framed as choices, and that choices be made.

- It establishes a common understanding of, and support for, the direction of the organization.

It is obvious that if a process of planning is to succeed, all involved should agree that it is needed and worth the time and trouble it will require. If such a consensus does not exist, the chief executive, senior staff, and key trustees will need to take time to ensure that one is developed. The chief executive has a special role, for if he or she does not take planning seriously, few others will see any reason to do so. Therefore, the chief executive must visibly lead and support the process. In the larger institutions, the executive will need to delegate day-to-day responsibility for planning but should be present at most of the planning meetings. At the smaller institutions, the chief executive will be the principal planner. Unless a strategic plan has been developed immediately prior to the arrival of a new chief executive, the process described below should be initiated.

Many books have described how to conduct planning in non-profit organizations; an excellent one is *Strategic Planning for Public and Nonprofit Organizations* by John M. Bryson (1988). This chapter follows his approach but emphasizes the role of the chief executive. Bryson makes the point that the purpose of planning is to define the basis for thinking and acting; planning is not the end but the means. Therefore, when enough thinking has been done to reveal appropriate actions, it is not necessary to wait until the entire process is complete before beginning to act.

The stages in the planning process are presented below in a logical order, but the exact sequence is less important than that the work be done in a natural and effective way, which will vary with the organization and the times.

Mission

Certainly the most fundamental point to be made about nonprofits is that they exist for one reason only: to fulfill a mission. "The mission statement [serves] a function akin to the profit motive in the private business world" (Knauft, Berger, and Gray, 1991, p. 119). Drucker (1989) underscores the importance of mission:

> Starting with the mission . . . focuses the organization on action . . . defines the specific strategies needed to attain crucial goals [and] creates a disciplined organization. It alone can prevent the most common degenerative disease of organizations: splintering their always limited resources on things that are "interesting" or look "profitable" rather than concentrating them on a very small number of productive efforts [p. 89].

It is easy for staff and board members to take the mission for granted: "We all know why we are here—let's get on with it" is a common view. For the new leader, this is a way to miss an important opportunity and possibly a danger as well. The recent literature on nonprofit leadership emphasizes the importance of mission not only to the organization but to the successful chief executive. "The most fundamental way in which leaders create commitment to a purpose is by defining what that purpose is" (Lynch, 1993, p. 66).

Planning therefore should start with a reexamination of the mission, which it should be possible to state in one paragraph. Although an institution's mission should remain constant over many years, it is still appropriate for an incoming chief executive to oversee a careful review of the existing statement. One that has not been examined in some time will often prove in need of revision; if it does not, that too will be a useful conclusion.

The statement should describe *what* the organization wants to accomplish and *why* rather than merely *how* it intends to go about it. It should focus on desired outcomes, not merely on good intentions. Mission statements that merely express intent raise no interesting questions and tend to bind the organization to the current set of activities, thereby promoting the status quo (Lynch, 1993). Since nonprofits exist solely to fulfill a mission, and since success can be measured only by the extent to which they do so, a clear, functional mission statement is critical to success and to the demonstration of success.

Here is an example of an ineffective statement: "The mission of the Gotham City Science Museum is to provide quality museum experiences to the people of the region." This statement is vague about what the museum will do, does not explain why, and offers no hint as to how success will be determined. The mission will be fulfilled if some reasonable number of people attend and if it plausibly can be claimed that they had a "quality experience." No one is required to act or to think differently.

A more useful statement might read: "To help achieve a scientifically literate society, the mission of the Gotham City Science

Museum is to enhance public understanding and awareness of science and technology, to do so for increasing numbers of the public, and to form partnerships that will aid the citywide and national effort to reform science education." This statement indicates what the museum will do and why and suggests that its success in achieving the mission could be subject to measurement.

Unfortunately, many mission statements have a generic sameness. However, with enough work and thought, a well-phrased mission description can be crafted to fit each organization. It is important not to rush through this work; otherwise, fundamental disagreements as to purpose can go undetected, only to rear up later and set the process back. Do not dismiss the mission statement as unworthy of effort—make sure that it becomes worthy. Involve senior officers of the organization, faculty if at an academic institution, trustees, and others as appropriate. Have the mission description approved by the board. If you do not, trouble can ensue, as at this nonprofit:

> At the time of transition to a new director, the board of an arts organization failed to take the time to discuss its mission and direction. The appointee and the board subsequently turned out to have quite different ideas as to the most appropriate purpose of the organization. "After a tumultuous period, the board decided to retain the original mission . . . it replaced the new director" [Knauft, Berger, and Gray, p. 5].

SWOT

Having defined or reaffirmed the mission, next assess the internal operation of the organization and identify the external factors that will affect the achievement of the mission. An effective technique is to go on a retreat off-site to conduct a "SWOT" exercise in which the Strengths and Weaknesses of the organization, which are to be found internally, and the Opportunities and Threats originating from the outside are identified. (Of course, these categories overlap—an item may appear to be both a threat and a weakness, for example—but remember that the goal is not to produce an impeccable taxonomy but to make sure that nothing important is overlooked.)

You may wish to use an outside facilitator at this retreat, but take no chances; only an expert will be able to help you. Plan the retreat carefully, leaving time for the attendees to get to know each other better. Send out any appropriate materials in advance. The chief executive should explain the purpose and format of the retreat, after which one to two hours should be spent on each of the four components of the SWOT exercise. Conducted properly, the retreat will not only provide much useful information but will enhance group spirit and cohesion. Everyone will return better informed about the organization, friendlier toward their colleagues, and with a renewed spirit of optimism and dedication.

Vision

Although change is always resisted, to engage in planning is to accept that at least some change is necessary and desirable: what is a plan but a description of a different and better way of doing things? When conducted properly, planning can set the stage for true institutional revitalization. But for that to occur, staff and trustees must be able to envision the organization succeeding at a much higher level. A well-defined and accepted mission statement and a rigorous SWOT assessment are essential but not visionary. The mission statement shows purpose and intent; the vision defines the successful accomplishment of the mission in a transcendent way that captures and stretches the imagination and commitment of all. Although the vision statement is introduced at this stage in the planning process, it could come at almost any time, from the beginning to the end.

Although a functional strategic plan—one that tells people what they should do next—can be established without a vision, it is doubtful that support for major organizational changes can come in its absence. To persuade people to change, they must see and hear a compelling revelation of how the organization, and their professional lives, can be distinctly better. As Lynch put it, "Without [a shared vision], work is just something to do to finance people's weekends" (1993, p. 78).

The vision statement will be one of the most important documents in the term of any chief executive; do not delegate or give away that responsibility. On the other hand, a vision developed in the dark by the chief executive without consultation would be suspect and fail to receive support. After all, any plan must be implemented ultimately by those who work at the institution. A vision statement uninformed by the views of key individuals and constituencies would soon be shelved. The real test of leadership is to produce a vision for the organization that would result in positive change *and* would find broad acceptance.

The one thing that the chief executive should not do is turn the vision statement over to a standing committee: pigs do not fly and standing committees do not envision; by their very nature they tend not to stray far from the accepted present, balancing competing interests and protecting the status quo. The executive should hand-pick a small, representative, and respected group to draw up a draft vision statement, with the executive acting as its chair and principal drafter. This group could be a subset of the planning committee, but the chief executive must have the final authority over the statement that emerges.

Strategic Issues

With a mission statement, a completed SWOT exercise, and an accepted vision statement, it is now possible to identify what Bryson (1988) calls the strategic issues—those fundamental choices that must be made if the vision is to be achieved. Every organization constantly faces choices, some minor in consequence and some major; often decisions are made before the options are clearly identified and thought through. The institution may be in such a rut that it does not even realize that it has certain choices. Perhaps the most useful feature of planning is that it forces choices to be specified explicitly. Unless that is done, incorrect choices, or no choices, may be made.

But if identifying the strategic issues is the most important stage of strategic planning, it may also be the most difficult. If the leader of the planning process is not careful and diligent, what starts out as an effort to frame choices will devolve into the raising of vague and unanswerable questions. As noted, raising the right questions is fundamental, but they must lead toward action, toward the selection of one option over others. With hard work and tough discipline, the planning committee can identify these strategic issues. Some examples may clarify:

1. A museum is breaking even financially but has little in the way of "internal venture capital." If attendance could be increased, there would be little marginal cost and most of the new revenue would become available. Considering the competing claims on its resources, should the museum increase its advertising budget?

2. A university finds its enrollment dropping and can no longer support all existing departments. Should it spend more money on recruitment or accept the losses and shrink?

3. A library has an opportunity to make its card catalogue available on the Internet, but doing so would be expensive. Is the network connection consistent with, or required by, its mission?

4. A small social service agency that is largely dependent on grants finds the competition increasing. Should it hire a professional development officer, rely on consultants, or continue to try to do the job itself?

The planning committee is likely to spend more time on defining and sorting the strategic issues than on anything else. Once the list is clearly spelled out, the committee may wish to rank the items in order of importance. Through such a winnowing and refining process, a set of priorities and natural grouping of strategic issues will gradually emerge. The next step is to begin to turn the planning process toward action.

Goals, Strategies, and Benchmarks

By this stage, the key strategies will have begun to fall together naturally under broad headings that can form the major goals of the plan. Goals should number fewer than ten and ideally no more than five or six. Each might have one to five accompanying strategies, and each of them should have several benchmarks: specific tasks to be completed by a specified date.

The chief executive and the planners should take the position that if it is not possible to state a goal and a set of strategies in such a way that the organization will know whether and when they have been achieved, by definition they cannot be part of a strategic plan. What good is a strategy whose success can never be determined? For example, to say that "the institution will achieve excellence by the year 2000" is not worth the ink to print it. Further, whenever possible, benchmarks should identify outcomes, not inputs.

As examples, let us assume that certain choices had been made by each of the four institutions used as illustrations above. Four corresponding benchmarks might be:

1. Benchmark: within x years, the advertising budget will have increased by 20 percent and attendance will have risen by 10 percent.

2. Benchmark: within x years, the university will have reduced its size by 5 percent while maintaining a balanced budget in each of the intervening years.

3. Benchmark: within x years, the card catalogue of the library will be on the Internet and fully supported.

4. Benchmark: within *x* years, the agency will have hired a professional development consultant and its annual total for gifts and grants will have increased by 10 percent.

Listing benchmarks is obviously a critical phase of planning and must be approached with care and rigor. It is easy to write down an overly ambitious set that proves impossible to meet. When more than a few are not met, the institution and the chief executive will be regarded properly as having failed. The benchmarks should stretch the organization's ability to meet them, but not to the breaking point.

Since the chief executive has primary responsibility for implementation of the plan, it is critical that he or she be fully committed to the achievement of each goal, strategy, and benchmark. Matters that do not rank highly in importance or that will be accomplished in any case should not take up space in the plan. A benchmark that does not have a reasonable probability of being reached should not be listed; ones that the chief executive does not want to become part of the agenda should be excluded.

After the strategies and benchmarks have been thoroughly discussed and resolved, one carefully chosen member of the planning team should draft the strategic plan itself. This could be the chief executive, but if not, the chief executive must have veto power. Inevitably, the executive will have responsibility for the plan and therefore must have concomitant authority. The draft plan should be critically reviewed by the planning team and approved as necessary by various constituent groups. Once improvements to it have been made, it should be adopted by the board.

Action

As Bryson (1988) notes, it is thinking and acting that are important, not planning. Plans that are not action oriented—that offer no hint as to what to do next—lie on the shelf. One recalls the Ford administration's effort toward reducing inflation: have everyone wear buttons proclaiming "WIN" for "whip inflation now." Pre-dictably, this novel strategy had no effect. If planning is to be worth anything, it must cause a change in the way people behave, from the chief executive on down.

Thus, the final stage of planning is the most important: with the plan, including benchmarks, adopted, each unit or department must now develop its own action plan for achieving those benchmarks that apply to it. These should be as concrete as any other part of the exercise. The planning committee should be satisfied that these plans are realistic and that a sufficient effort will be made to see that they are achieved. These action plans can then be used in annual budgeting and in departmental performance review.

Once the strategic plan is implemented, planning should con-tinue, now shifting into a monitoring mode, with assumptions and strategies revised as necessary. A senior staff member (at the smaller institutions, the chief executive) must have responsibility for plan-ning and monitoring. In several years, the planning process should again go into high gear and a new strategic plan, incorporating new facts about the environment and the organization, should be pro-duced. Planning is a continual process; once an organization has begun, it will indeed prove indispensable.

Quality Management

The mind recoils from the memory of the many managerial tech-niques that have arrived with fanfare over the last few decades, among them management by objectives, the managerial grid, pro-gram-planning-budgeting systems, zero-based budgeting, one-minute management, the search for excellence. Most have fallen by the wayside; some of the companies extolled have gone bankrupt; some of the corporate chief executives singled out for praise are in prison. Caveat emptor.

Within the last several years, another innovation has appeared. Like so many, it was invented in the United States, grew to prominence in Japan, and has now been reimported. This is Total Quality Management, or TQM, which has worked, and worked on a large scale: its use has in part led to the transfer of market share or indeed of whole markets from one country to another. The Japanese were the first to apply the advice of the late W. Edwards Deming that corporations should discover what their customers want and try to provide it with maximum efficiency. As a result, many Japanese corporations redesigned their operations from the ground up. Their success in using what has come to be called Total Quality Management is history. More recently, application of these principles has transformed several major U.S. companies, including Ford, Xerox, Motorola, and Federal Express.

The premise of TQM is that organizations do best over the long run when they concentrate not on making a profit—or in the case of a nonprofit on balancing the budget with a bit left over—but on the needs of their customers. The key is that an organization that focuses overly on its short-term finances will take actions to increase its profits or its surplus that prove detrimental in the long run. On the other hand, a company or nonprofit that puts its effort into finding out what the customer wants and providing it with the greatest efficiency and highest quality at the lowest possible cost—that organization has laid the foundation for a generation of financial success and mission fulfillment.

The need for attention to quality and efficiency arises because in any organization the work product is the result of a set of procedures, some of whose details may not have been reviewed for a long time. These procedures have evolved over years or even decades as a result of the whims and beliefs of past managers. No one could possibly reconstruct their history now or justify each step. Unless an organization has tried TQM or something like it, few of its procedures will have had a rigorous, step-by-step analysis.

Organizations that have used TQM have discovered that a high percentage of errors—as many as 85 percent—arise not because of the incorrect implementation of correct procedures but because the procedures themselves are wrong or inefficient (Chaffee and Sherr, 1993). Given the level of their training and the clarity of their instructions, people are found to be performing about as well as they can. As procedures are improved and replaced, errors decline and the organization can turn more of its resources toward better training.

Why do such inefficient procedures arise? Parkinson (1957) observed that organizations inevitably become more and more complex, adding new staff and increasing administrative levels. A problem is corrected not by going back to square one and redesigning but by adding a fix in the form of an additional step or layer of bureaucracy. Over time, presumed fixes accrete until procedures become encrusted and inefficient, sometimes existing more to serve the convenience of staff than the organization's constituency. Eventually, processes are marked by the need to "rework" (repair earlier mistakes) and to "scrap" (discard completed work and start over) and by "unnecessary complexity" (steps that add no value). The goal of TQM is to eliminate each of the three by examining procedures in detail, asking whether and how each step does or does not add value from the point of view of its beneficiary, or customer. (Note that in TQM lingo, a customer is anyone with whom a person in the organization has a business interaction. A customer is not only the person who buys a ticket to a museum, pays tuition to a university, or checks out a book from a library; it is also a co-worker who needs a service or information, another office within the organization, donors, vendors, suppliers, trustees. If the word *customer* offends or seems not to apply, substitute another of your choice. The point is that nonprofits exist for the benefit of someone other than their own staffs and boards; the mission statement should make it clear who it is.)

Nonprofits need to try TQM because most have not considered that they have "customers" in the broad sense defined above. In the business world, competition ensures that companies providing the least quality for the cost will fail. But nonprofits have not been perceived as competing directly with each other and therefore may have gotten away longer with overgrown bureaucracies and encrusted practices. However, nonprofits would be foolhardy to presume that they do not have inefficiencies and mistakes to rival those of corporations. Most of us have little trouble thinking immediately of a procedure or two at our organization that appears to take an unreasonably long time or is not sufficiently customer oriented. Since TQM requires the establishment of a clear mission, has as its end the satisfaction of clients (customers, beneficiaries), and depends on staff who want to do a better job, all characteristics of nonprofits, the opportunity may be especially great in the nonprofit sector.

In summary, TQM has these features:

- "Customer" needs identified
- Staff from the chief executive on down committed to continuous improvement at all levels
- Careful analysis of key procedures for errors and bottlenecks
- Improvements made promptly
- Funds allocated for staff training

How could an approach based on these steps not be worth trying?

Implementing TQM

To get started, many organizations, if they do not have the expertise internally, will wish to bring in a consultant to explain and promote the process to their staff and perhaps to members of their board. Ask colleagues for advice about consultants they have used and interview several, but be careful that the style of the consultant fits with that of your organization. For example, a small nonprofit will gain little from a consultant whose experience is with larger companies and whose speech is filled with the all-too-prevalent jargon of TQM. Remember that anyone can call him- or herself a consultant; make more than one reference check! As Niels Bohr said, "An expert is a [person] who has made all the mistakes which can be made in a very narrow field" (quoted in Mackay, 1977, p. 22).

One advantage of TQM is that it is simple enough to be easily tested. Pick a process that needs improvement (but not one that is too complex or large) and give it a try. Select a team to analyze the procedures; include people who are part of the process and some who are not. Interview each person who has a role and make a flowchart showing each step and how long it takes. Be sure to include the actual steps and timetable, not the theoretical ones. Identify where the breakdowns and bottlenecks occur and fix them. Use the TQM approach of "plan-do-check-act": study a process and figure out how to improve it; test the improvement; monitor the results to see that improvement actually results; if it does, put the improvement into place permanently. Once TQM has worked in one example, communicate your success throughout the organization and find another on which to try it.

Case Study: Exhibit Repair at a Science Museum

Science museums today base their exhibits on the principle that people learn best by doing. Thus, they design exhibits that are interactive. This is all very well until one realizes that a large museum may have a million visitors or more annually, with as many as one-third to one-half of them children. As ten, then a hundred, then a thousand children pull a given lever or push a given button in a museum exhibit on a single day, only the most robust devices will still be working by day's end. Thus, the design, construction, and maintenance of exhibits is crucial; one nonworking exhibit may equal hundreds or thousands of dissatisfied customers. Museums do not need to do sophisticated audience surveys to know that having well-designed, educational exhibits that work is the single most important factor in the fulfillment of their mission and in their financial success.

The Franklin Institute, a large science museum in Philadelphia, found itself unable in spite of its best efforts to reduce the number of complaints about broken exhibits and decided to use exhibit maintenance as a way to learn about the methods of TQM. A team composed of some who worked directly in the exhibit maintenance department and some from outside was selected to analyze problems and propose solutions. They identified the most significant causes of inadequate exhibit maintenance:

- Complicated management processes including bottlenecks

- Insufficient number of technicians

- Lack of training for technical staff

- Insufficient documentation

- Poor design of exhibits that subsequently caused them to break down more easily or be more difficult to maintain

- Inadequate reporting of broken exhibits

Note that these flaws all lie with the system and not with the individuals who operate it.

A second set of causes was thought to be less significant:

- Insufficient funds to reengineer exhibits that are especially prone to breaking down

- Advanced age of many exhibits

- Abuse endured by the exhibits, especially when the floor staff is shorthanded

- Poor communication

The immediate conclusion from this analysis was that the weaknesses identified in the first set—management, training, documentation, design, reporting—all fall within a realm in which improvement is possible: they can be fixed. The problems in the second set, with the exception of poor communication, are the hard facts with which most science museums must live today. Had it been the other way round, TQM might have had little to add to the improvement of exhibit maintenance.

Next the team charted the flow of the procedures that the museum employs in exhibit maintenance and repair. No one present had been fully aware of the complexity of the process taken as a whole. The overall system was found to comprise four major components and four subcomponents; the total number of steps in all the procedures taken together was 104. Those who were familiar with the process had been aware that all exhibit maintenance and repair work flowed through one person, but the extent to which this constituted a bottleneck was not fully apparent until the flowchart was prepared. Even though this individual was hardworking and effective, he was not superhuman. Obviously, procedures had to be improved.

A key to TQM—one that Deming stressed—is the need for measurement. Unless one can measure the quality of a process *before* improvements are attempted, one will not know how well those improvements have worked. (Indeed, Deming was trained as a statistical analyst of manufacturing procedures.) To know whether the team's work on exhibit maintenance led to improvement required a baseline against which future results could be compared. Although an analysis of exhibit maintenance could be done in a more sophisticated way, this team decided on a simple approach: each member chose ten exhibits of different types in different areas of the museum, visited that exhibit at definite intervals, and reported on a specific form whether the exhibit was broken. This "snapshot" analysis revealed that approximately 70 percent of exhibits were

working at the time they were visited. For adequate visitor satisfaction and good word-of-mouth advertising, that figure needed to be
substantially higher.

The team submitted these recommendations:

- Change management procedures to eliminate the
  bottleneck.

- Provide technicians with better training, particularly in
  problem solving skills, thereby allowing them to work
  more independently.

- Revise the process by which museum staff examine
  exhibits and report problems.

- Make all documentation available to technicians.

- Require representation and sign-offs from those who
  design and build exhibits, as well from as those who
  will operate, maintain, and explain them.

- If funds can be found, increase management staff so
  that one staff member can focus on long-range and
  reengineering issues while the other manages day-to-
  day work.

- If funds can be found, reengineer certain important but
  fragile exhibits to make them more robust.

As a result of the continuing effort of this TQM team, the
process was considerably streamlined. Steps were cut in half; more
exhibits were "up"; repairs are more lasting as technicians gain
know-how and confidence. Of course, the skeptic will say, all this
resulted merely from the application of common sense and discipline and could have been done without TQM. That is true, but it
had not been.

Convergence of TQM and Planning

Strategic planning and Total Quality Management both derive from the mission of the organization and a focus on process and are based on information. TQM posits that the mission can only be understood through a detailed knowledge of the organization's customers and their needs and expectations. Planning is directed toward longer-range goals; TQM aims at continuous improvement in quality of services or products. A major difference is that TQM teams always include those who will implement the change or perform the work; strategic planning committees often are composed of higher-level staff. Clearly, the two approaches can and often should be used in tandem, as each can strengthen the other. To be effective, both must have the public, enthusiastic, and constant support of the chief executive.

8

Using Evaluation to
Confirm Mission Success

Trust, but verify.

Russian saying

On August 3, 1993, Congress passed a bill that will have far-reaching implications for almost every nonprofit organization. The Government Performance and Results Act (GPRA) directs each federal agency to adopt a number of administrative tools, including multiyear strategic plans, annual performance plans, and annual performance reports. To comply, each federal agency henceforth will have to evaluate its programs. As one way of gaining information, agencies with grant programs will turn to their grantees for their own evaluations of projects funded by the agency. Few nonprofits are not to some degree—perhaps indirectly—the beneficiary of the programs of the federal agencies covered under GPRA, and few will fail to feel its effects. Already the grant application forms of many federal programs require a description of how the project would be evaluated. Not only government agencies but corporate and private foundations as well increasingly require that the projects they support be evaluated. Soon proposals to any funder, government or private, will not only have to include a section on evaluation, they will be judged as much on the quality of that section as on any other.

The Case for Evaluation

As mission-driven organizations, nonprofits should be engaging in serious evaluation whether or not they are prodded to do so by agencies and foundations. They have no other way of knowing whether they are fulfilling their missions. A company succeeds if it earns a profit and thereby returns value to its shareholders. It may require a great deal of hard and clever work for it to do so, but knowing whether it has or has not succeeded at this fundamental objective is a routine matter of financial reporting (this is not to say that some creative accounting and reporting techniques are not used in both sectors). To make the same determination for a non-profit is much more difficult. One cannot find the answer in a financial report: finance is only the means, not the end. For a complex set of reasons, however, most nonprofits have not performed evaluations:

- Until recently, seldom has anyone asked them to do so.

- They have not known how.

- They have believed that much of what happens in the nonprofit world is not amenable to evaluation. (And sometimes they are right.)

- They have been fearful of a negative result—or none at all.

- Taking time out for evaluation seems only to delay getting on with the real job at hand.

These reasons are all quite understandable; some are serious concerns that will be addressed in the rest of this chapter. But no longer do any suffice to defend the absence of evaluation. The chief executive has a special interest because evaluation measures change. But most nonprofits and their chief executives have little experience with evaluation, and many staff members are apt not to understand its importance. Reasons like those above can always be found to forgo evaluation or to minimize its importance. Evaluation is apt to happen routinely and to be done well only if the chief executive explains why it must.

Evaluation need not be costly: funders will often pay for it. Many now insist that every proposal include a description of how the project will be evaluated and they allow a budget for evaluation to be included. Stevens, Lawrenz, and Sharp (1994), speaking for the National Science Foundation Directorate of Education and Human Resources, write that as a rough rule of thumb, evaluation should amount to 5 to 10 percent of project costs for larger projects; for smaller ones, the percentage may need to be higher. Most agencies and foundations will not balk at providing such a percentage in the project budget.

Institutional Evaluation

The overarching evaluative question naturally has to do with the effectiveness of the institution as a whole. Is it achieving its mission? Are resources being wisely used? Is it engaged in planning and reasonably prepared for the future? These larger questions are of course the most difficult; nevertheless, a great deal can be learned.

For some nonprofits, typically the larger ones, institutional evaluation is not a choice: it is required in order for the institution to be accredited. Museums, academic institutions, hospitals—all are reviewed by professional organizations or commissions and granted accreditation or not. In a typical accreditation review, the institution spends several months preparing a self-study. This report is sent to a team of expert reviewers who use it as the basis for a visit of several days during which they conduct interviews and hold meetings. The team then writes up its own report and submits it to the accrediting agency with a recommendation. The board of the accrediting agency considers the recommendation and makes a final judgment.

Accreditation might be awarded for a longer or a shorter period, with required intermediate reports or smaller-scale visits.

Many smaller nonprofits are not subject to the obligation and the opportunity afforded by accreditation, yet they too can and should have an institutional evaluation performed. Some belong to professional associations that have voluntary but formalized evaluation programs serving the same purpose. Any organization can conduct a self-study and bring in a team of experts. Consultants can easily be found by contacting a professional association or a sister institution. United Way, Business Volunteers for the Arts, the local grantmakers' forum, universities, and others can provide the needed expertise. O'Connell (1993) advises that in every town there are many successful nonprofit leaders who would be proud to be asked. The new *Drucker Foundation Self-Assessment Tool for Nonprofit Organizations* (Peter F. Drucker Foundation for Nonprofit Management, 1993) is an excellent and inexpensive way to launch the process. Strategic planning includes an overall assessment of institutional effectiveness, beginning with the mission statement and proceeding through the SWOT exercise and on to the plan itself. Thus, it includes a useful evaluative component. In short, there is no scarcity of ways by which an institution can gain an overview of its effectiveness in meeting its goals. Chief executives and boards should insist that such reviews be carried out every few years.

Departmental Evaluation

Whereas it may be going too far to say that an institution is no stronger than its weakest component, some administrative departments are so critical that their operation must be a top priority. For example, few nonprofits can succeed without a first-class program of fundraising. For another, if the finance office does not manage and invest funds properly, some will be wasted and confidence in the institution will be diminished. Thus, it is essential that the chief executive ensure that these and other critical departments operate professionally and ideally at a high level of excellence. To ensure that they do, these departments must be evaluated periodically. The same general approach as used in an accreditation review can be applied. First, a self-study is prepared, where appropriate using the services of a consultant. The self-study includes comparable data from other institutions or from the field at large. This self-study is reviewed in draft form by senior administrators and if necessary sent back for further work. Then an individual expert or a small team studies the report and visits to interview staff within the department and as appropriate those outside it. The team prepares a confidential report for the chief executive. The chief executive should select this team with the advice and concurrence of staff within the department, using contacts in professional associations or general knowledge of the people in the field. They should be asked to make recommendations based on the present level of funding of the department.

A difficulty can arise when members of a department selected by the chief executive for outside review feel singled out and threatened. Therefore, it is critical that reviews not be conducted only when a department is perceived to be in trouble or when it is believed by the chief executive to need new leadership. Some reviews should take place when the executive has made a commitment to strengthen an area and wants outside advice as to how best to go about it. It is also helpful if the chief executive frames at least some of the questions that the departmental review is expected to answer and makes sure that some are positive and encouraging. Finally, the executive might wish to announce that over a period of a few years each department will be reviewed.

Departments That Deal in Numbers

Some departments resemble a company in that they do have a "bottom line," a target number or set of numbers that they are expected to meet. Social service agencies can count the number of clients served in various programs or the number who have successfully "graduated" and no longer need the service. The development department, no matter how small, should have dollar targets. In a college, the admissions department should have a goal for the number of new freshmen. For departments where such numerical goals are available, it is a simple matter to tell whether they were met. Even when they were, however, plenty of room for improvement may still exist: for example, it may now be clear that last year's target was too low and that the department should be expected to meet a higher one.

When targets are not met, it is seldom easy to determine why and what to do about it, for the success of a given department hardly ever depends on its own efforts alone. For example, whether fundraising targets are achieved depends not only on the efforts of development staff but on the willingness of the chief executive and board members to give of their own time and to "make the ask"; on the strength of the board overall; and on the economy.

Lynch (1993) suggests that staff be asked to set their own targets; most of the time, after thinking over the options, they will choose a goal that is as high as or higher than one the supervisor would have proposed. If not, the supervisor can always overrule. Lynch also makes the critical point that people perform better and gain more satisfaction when they are held to higher standards.

As an example of the evaluation of a department that deals in numbers, let us examine in more depth the assessment of the fundraising department.

Fundraising Department

Most institutions set a target for fundraising that is based on historical trends and then set about to meet it. Failure to do so is often attributed to various environmental factors beyond the institution's control. If the target is met, everyone breathes a collective sigh of relief and is satisfied. As Greenfield (1993) puts it, "Only a few organizations know their potential, much less their capacity, because they use fund-raising only as a means to realizing a targeted amount of money" (p. 649). A thorough analysis of the environment for fundraising and an evaluation of the quality of the fundraising effort can pave the way for an institution to come much closer to reaching its potential.

When should the new chief executive consider conducting an evaluation of fundraising performance? I recommend that it be done within the first six months, for the following reasons: (1) Fundraising is vital, and as soon as possible you need to know how well it is being done. (2) The study will allow you to evaluate the development staff. Should you need new leadership, the sooner you find it out the better. (3) No one, including the development staff, will be in the least surprised if the chief executive asks for an evaluation early on. Indeed, trustees and others will applaud the action. The same step taken a year or two later could be regarded as a vote of no confidence in the staff.

Before proceeding with an evaluation of fundraising operations, the chief executive and board need to have some idea of the potential provided by the type of institution they serve. Religious organizations receive the bulk of gifts, followed by human services, education, and health. Next come the arts and culture, and finally civic and public benefit causes. An institution should aspire to be among the leaders for its type, but a small arts organization can never raise as much money as a college with a large alumni base and in all likelihood much greater longevity and visibility in the community.

As a first step in evaluating the fundraising department, hire a well-qualified outside consultant. Doing so has several advantages over conducting the evaluation internally. A good consultant will be objective and will be perceived as objective, two different but equally important attributes. A consultant can ask tougher questions than anyone inside the institution. Finally, a good consultant has a field of view that is much broader than anyone internally could have, allowing the institution (and staff) to be compared with many others. Professional associations, funders, and colleagues can recommend names of potential consultants. Two or three should be brought in for interviews and one selected. A contract should be signed and deadlines set.

As the process is getting underway, all available data on fundraising should be assembled, including the following:

- Comparable information from other institutions and from the profession at large. Professional associations and fundraising organizations—for example, the Council for the Advancement and Support of Education, the American Association of Fund-Raising Counsel, the INDEPENDENT SECTOR, the Indiana University Center on Philanthropy, and others—can supply such information or help to locate it.

- The fundraising record by type of gift (annual fund versus endowment), by source (trustee versus member or alumnus), by size, and so forth.

- The number of fundraising events and their attendance.

- The size and success of the last capital campaign (if any) and whether pledges are still to be paid.

- Historical trends in each category.

- The size and qualifications of the development staff compared with national norms.

In the midst of all the data that will be assembled, as Greenfield (1993, pp. 667–673) notes, certain questions in particular reveal whether the institution is healthy, growing, and broadly supported:

- How many new donors gave in the past year?

- How many who gave the year before gave again last year and how many did so at a higher level?

- How many board members gave to annual operations and at what level? What percentage of the board gave last year and the year before? What percentage has never given?

- For an institution with members, such as a museum or library, what is the trend and how many repeat from year to year? For a college, what percentage of alumni gave last year and has the percentage been growing? How does the percentage who gave and the average gift compare with similar institutions?

- Has the size of the development staff been stable, growing, or declining? What kind of reports does the department regularly provide the chief executive and the board?

Finally comes the question of productivity compared with national norms. Given the number of institutions that engage in fundraising and have for many decades, a great deal of collective information is available. An institution with a fundraising program more than two years old (long enough for its success to be measured) or that has had new leadership for that long or longer can perform a cost-benefit analysis and compare its results with those of the profession at large. For example, as the roughest measure, the Council of Better Business Bureaus, Inc. has proposed that the cost of a mature fundraising program should not exceed 35 percent of the amount raised: to raise $100,000, an institution should not have to spend more than $35,000. If it does spend more, either it has the wrong staff or it is relying too heavily on relatively unproductive methods such as direct mail (see below).

Perhaps the most successful and most mature fundraising programs are found at the Ivy League universities. In a noncampaign period, when all gifts are included, the costs of such a program will run to 7 to 8 percent of revenue generated. In a major campaign period when all gifts are included, even with added expenditures of a campaign, costs will average 5 to 6 percent. That is a goal to which all nonprofits can aspire. Pocock (1989) surveyed some twelve hundred academic institutions and found that the average amount spent per dollar raised was 22 percent. However, the schools with the *lowest* ratio of costs to money raised spent *more* on fundraising in total than the average. In other words, these institutions spent more but they also raised even more proportionately—more than enough to offset the extra expenditure and to lower their percentage cost. This study may contain a lesson for other nonprofits.

Table 1 can serve as a basis for comparison:

Direct mail is expensive and overreliance on it will cost more than it is worth. On the other hand, once begun, it may be cost-effective to obtain renewals by direct mail. Corporate, foundation, and planned giving are productive methods. Benefit events such as an annual gala or dinner are difficult to assess. Some experts believe that if the staff and volunteer time and the opportunity cost are all taken into account, few such events would prove worth the time and effort. On the other hand, for some trustees and volunteers, the annual ball is the highlight of a year's service; were it to be eliminated, so would their interest. Smaller nonprofits may need to do somewhat better than 50 percent of gross or net on benefit events, as this example suggests:

> The new executive director of a social service agency found that the agency had added more and more special events without giving careful thought to the net amount raised. The director instituted a policy whereby each proposed new special event was required to have the potential to raise more money than the least productive event currently being conducted. If it did so, the new event would replace the less productive one. Thus, the least effective special events were weeded out.

A capital campaign is the most productive technique, but the estimate of cost given in the table is based on campaigns that were

Table 1. Reasonable Fundraising Guidelines.

Method	Cost/dollar raised[a]	Cost/dollar raised[b]
Direct mail acquisition	$1.00 to $1.25	$1.50
Direct mail renewal	0.20	0.20
Benefit events	50% of gross	50% of net
Corporations and foundations	0.20	0.10
Planned giving	0.25	0.25
Capital campaigns	0.05 to 0.10	0.05 to 0.15

[a]Greenfield, 1993
[b]Howe, 1991

carefully timed and planned and that succeeded. "A capital campaign . . . must . . . represent the studied conclusion that all traditional funding options have been exhausted and a capital drive is now required to raise most or all of the money needed by a certain date" (Greenfield, 1991, p. 17).

Finally, the table demonstrates that overall fundraising costs, derived from a variety of the techniques shown in the table depending on the maturity of the program, should not exceed, say, 25 to 30 percent. If the costs at your institution do, something is wrong that needs to be corrected.

Project Evaluation

When most of us think of evaluation, we envision a measure to determine retrospectively the degree of success of a project. In keeping an eye on how well the organization is meeting its mission objectives, however, the chief executive needs to be aware that this retrospective evaluation is logically the last of a three-stage process.

Planning Evaluation

Rossi and Freeman (1993) make a strong case for having evaluators participate in the design of a project from the start. A good evaluator can ask the right questions at the right time, which is when the project is in its planning stages. For example, the evaluator can make sure that the following kinds of questions are addressed as the project is being developed:

How does it foster our mission? Why is this project being done, and why now? Why does it have a higher priority than others? What is it intended to accomplish? Who is the audience?

What resources—financial and human—will it require and how will they be allocated? How large is the budget and from where will the funds come? Is there a contingency budget? Will the project require the formal reassignment of staff or can it be done as part of regular duties?

Does it have all the formal approvals that it needs? Just to be on the safe side, should the board endorse the project? Should certain board committees be made aware of it?

What is the timeline for the project? Given experience with similar ones, is the timeline reasonable? Who will manage the project and what tools will they need?

What information does past research and experience provide that will enhance the project? If it is an educational project, does it use what is known about how people learn in that setting? For example, if it is a museum exhibit, does it use the base of research information on how people learn in museums, which is different from the way they learn in classrooms?

How can we build into the project, in advance, features that will make it possible for it to be evaluated effectively once it is completed? What is the plan for evaluating the project? What things will be measured, how, and when? How will the data be collected? What level will various attributes have to reach before the project is deemed a success?

What are the expected and measurable outcomes? (If few worthy outcomes can be defined, choose another project on which to spend the institution's precious time and resources.) How will the project, if successful, be replicated both at our institution and where appropriate at others?

These are the very sorts of questions that are too often assumed to have been answered. In the rush of enthusiasm for O'Connell's "bright idea," those who conceived the idea can plunge ahead, leaving fundamental questions unanswered and jeopardizing the eventual success of the project. A neutral, objective evaluator can play devil's advocate, asking those awkward but essential questions that no one else may have the nerve to ask. Here is an example in which evaluators were not listened to until almost too late:

Science museums have learned that the button has the same irresistible appeal as Alice's bottle labeled "Drink Me." The Science Museum of Virginia opened a new exhibit called Balloon Ascent, in which a balloon was to slowly fill with hot air and then rise. As the balloon heated, a scale to which it was attached showed the upward pulling force; after it had inflated fully, the visitor was either to push a button marked "launch" or wait for an automatic launch. In spite of the urging of evaluators, initial prototyping of the exhibit dealt only with its mechanical operation and not with visitor behavior. When it opened, however, evaluators found that although 70 percent of the visitors read the exhibit label, most pushed the launch button long before the balloon was sufficiently inflated to rise. The designers and evaluators considered several options: speeding up the inflate cycle, rewriting the label yet again, or figuring out a way to make buttons work for the exhibit. Selecting the latter, they added a second button marked "heat," noting that "this change was easily implemented, since the heat button had no effect." Visitors dutifully pressed it first and then waited before pushing the launch button. The success rate doubled and the amount of time spent at the exhibit tripled. Eventually, in a spirit of complete honesty, the heat button was made to slightly accelerate the heating cycle (McNamara, 1991).

Formative Evaluation

The poet Robert Burns wrote, "The best laid schemes o' mice and men go oft awry" (1962, p. 27). No matter how careful an organization is in the planning and development of projects, and even if evaluators are present from the outset, plans will go awry. A host of unforeseen circumstances can arise, and some usually will, to cause a project not to work out as intended. Therefore, it is critical not to wait until a project is completed before evaluating it but to do so while it is underway, particularly in the early stages as information is beginning to arrive.

As a project is launched, a set of questions having to do with its implementation, rather than its preliminary success, needs to be asked:

- Have the promised resources been provided? Are the people who were to carry out the project committing the time that was expected?

- What unforeseen circumstances have arisen that need to be taken into account for the remainder of the project?

- Is the plan being followed? Is the project on schedule?

Next come questions that establish whether the project appears to be achieving its goals:

- From early returns, does it appear that the expected outcomes are taking place? If not, can effective corrections be made?

- Which parts of the project appear most successful and to need the least revision, and conversely?

- Does the project appear to have a reasonable chance of overall success? If not, and if its flaws cannot be corrected, how can the project be terminated with the least damage and at the lowest cost? How will the decision to terminate be communicated to the funders?

Careful attention to these sorts of questions will put the project in the best position to succeed.

Summative Evaluation

Finally we come to what is commonly understood to be evaluation: the answer to the question, did the project succeed? A sound summative, or retrospective, evaluation will include several questions such as these:

Did the project meet all of its goals? How do we know? If only some were met, which ones, and why?

What was learned, both positively and negatively, that had not been expected? Why were these outcomes not anticipated?

Did the project proceed and end on schedule and remain within budget and staffing allocations? If not, why not, and what was learned that can help future projects to do so?

Was the project worth its total cost? Total is emphasized because an accurate assessment needs to include not only the direct, budgeted expense but the indirect expense as well: the cost of all the many support services that any project requires, including the amount of staff time taken up. Finally, although it cannot be quantified, every activity has an opportunity cost: time and resources spent on it are not available for something else. The question of overall cost-effectiveness is, of course, both the most difficult to answer and the most important. It will need to be addressed by the chief executive and other leaders, using information made available through the evaluation; finally the decision will rest with the good judgment that the chief executive is being paid to provide.

How will the project be reported and (if appropriate) made available for replication elsewhere? Evaluation studies will do no good if they are not communicated, not read, not understood, or if they arrive too late.

These questions are the ones that will interest the chief executive, the funders, the board, and the public the most.

Choosing an Evaluator

If, as has been stressed, the evaluator is present from early in a project's development, that individual will have to be identified and available more or less permanently. Some large institutions can afford to have an expert evaluator as a permanent staff member. Medium-sized institutions might have a person who serves the function but who also has other responsibilities. Smaller nonprofits will have to contract for evaluation services (and all may wish to do so in certain instances) or call upon a local university for an evaluation volunteer. Professional and nonprofit associations can provide references. These organizations could also be of even more assistance, as this case suggests:

The Greater Gotham Cultural Alliance comprises over two hundred cultural and arts organizations in a major city. Concluding that evaluation was important and here to stay and recognizing that its constituent members had little knowledge about evaluation or money to spend on it, the GGCA established a relationship with a consulting firm that specialized in evaluation, paying an annual fee in return for a specified level of evaluation services to be provided to its members. The dues of each GGCA member rose slightly, but now each had available the services of expert evaluators who were generally familiar with their work and with the city.

Both internal and external evaluators have potential disadvantages. Internal evaluators may lack credibility with funders—a federal official was heard to say, "Internal evaluation is always suspect." Outside contractors must have clients and may be tempted to tell the current client what the contractor believes it wants to hear. In some cases, the internal evaluator could perform the planning and formative evaluations, with the final evaluation handled by an outside contractor. But in the end, the credibility of the institution will be at stake—it is up to the chief executive to ensure that evaluations are honest.

Characteristics of a Good Evaluation

To summarize, a credible and useful evaluation will be marked by these characteristics:

Its purpose and benefit have been communicated to the staff. It is understood by most that project evaluation is intended to help them to do a better job. Even if they do not agree, they still must participate.

A well-qualified evaluator is either present on the staff of the organization or available from outside, perhaps through the offices of a professional or nonprofit association. If from outside, this evaluator is already familiar with the organization and its mission and is broadly sympathetic and supportive. If the evaluator is internal, it is made clear that the messenger who brings bad tidings will not be penalized.

The evaluator is a member of the planning teams of the organization and routinely attends meetings at which new projects are discussed. The evaluator is neutral, dispassionate, and reports through appropriate channels, presenting recommendations for changes to project management, not to the subjects.

The evaluation is economical in that it tries to assess a small number of important questions rather than every question that can be imagined. Experience shows that evaluation is difficult enough even with a limited set of issues to address. Throw in the kitchen sink and nothing valuable may be learned.

It is accurate and objective. It does not tell management what it wants to hear unless it is right.

It is reported clearly, succinctly, and on time. It is understated in the way its conclusions are framed, preferring to claim too little than too much. It includes a one-page summary that allows the chief executive to learn all that is necessary to know about the project. It is distributed appropriately, ideally being made available to anyone inside or outside the institution who wishes to see it.

It may disappoint the chief executive and the project team, but it does not surprise them—they have been informed along the way about its progress. Whether the findings are going to be positive or negative, that information has already been conveyed to the chief executive. If they are negative, consideration has been given to how that result will be communicated to the funding agency.

All this puts a considerable burden on an internal evaluator, in time required if nothing else, and makes a strong case for using an external one at least some of the time.

The Elusive Final Answer

Although we would like to know with absolute certainty whether a project has succeeded, and exactly why, how much can we really expect to know? To be fair, and to use evaluation most effectively, the chief executive needs to have a firm grasp of the answer to this question, as do funders and boards. If we are to hold project planners and managers accountable, how much accountability can we fairly demand?

Whether a project succeeded, and why it did so or did not, are two separable questions; they are also by far the most difficult for evaluators to answer. Even if we stipulate that evaluations are conducted professionally, without serious flaws in design or implementation, limitations remain. One is that—given the complexity of human behavior—even when the desired results are obtained, we cannot always be sure of the reason. If participation was voluntary, those who signed up may have been predisposed to succeed. We do know that when the subjects of an evaluation are aware that it is being conducted, they often perform better.

A second limitation arises because any activity that lasts for more than a short while will likely be affected by a change in one or more important factors in its environment. For example, most educational enhancement projects, whether they occur in a school or off-site, are apt to be affected by other factors. Students are taking other subjects and being bombarded by all the demands placed on young people today. Many urban students change schools annually; substitute teachers arrive to replace the one under whom the project began; some other part of the curriculum is altered while the project is underway. A semester-long educational project in which no change occurred in any outside factor that might affect—whether positively or negatively—the outcome of the project would be rare indeed. This usually makes it impossible to say with certainty that a given effect occurred because and only because of the intervention of the particular project being evaluated. Often researchers attempt to get around this difficulty by establishing a control group, but this approach is not a panacea, having some of the same inherent problems. Further, in some cases it may be unethical to provide benefits to the group being studied while arbitrarily denying them to the control group.

The chief executive must see that evaluation is done but must also understand that a certain amount has to be taken on faith. As in the proverb with which this chapter opens, "Trust, but verify."

Part III

. . . .

Special Role of the Chief Executive

Nonprofits depend on the support of their various publics, to whom the chief executive is the key institutional representative. The ability of the executive to enlist the support necessary to provide the resources and the confidence for change depends greatly on the executive's ability to deliver an effective message. The great nonprofit leaders, like the great leaders in any field, have generally been great speakers. Not everyone can aspire to oratory, but anyone intelligent enough to be selected as a chief executive in the first place can become a good speaker merely by following a few simple rules.

Internal communication is a requisite for a successful organization. Without it, staff perform in relative isolation, unable to reinforce each other and unaware of how their work fits into the mission, the vision, and the plan. The chief executive can reap a large return from the investment of a small amount of time and effort in communicating with staff at all levels.

Financial health is vital. Since few or no nonprofits can balance their budgets entirely from earned income and program grants, they must depend sometimes heavily on philanthropy past and present. The chief executive is the key fundraiser and taking the long view, this is one of the most important duties of the executive. As with nearly everything in life, success at raising money is largely determined by hard work and common sense.

In their previous positions, most new chief executives have not had to deal directly with trustees. Absent their active and enthusiastic support, however, the executive will not only be without a platform for change but without a job. The board chair is the single most important person with whom the chief executive has to deal and a special relationship is required. Together, you and your board chair can bring about true and lasting change. If you are not together, change will prove elusive.

To all things there is a season. Many nonprofit executives, for a variety of reasons, last only two or three years in the position. Others are able to stay longer, five years and more. When the tenure begins to approach eight to ten years, however, the rate of change tends to diminish rapidly. Unfortunately, forces personal and professional conspire to prolong the tenure of many chief executives who have lasted that long or longer—which is well beyond the period during which they are able to be change agents. This is a personal tragedy for many chief executives and a problem for the entire sector; those who care about nonprofit institutions ought to find a way to help.

9

Communicating Effectively
with Staff and the Public

A [person] may lack everything but tact and convic-
tion and still be a forcible speaker; but without these
nothing will avail. . . . Fluency, grace, logical order,
and the like, are merely the decorative surface of ora-
tory.

Charles Horton Cooley,
Human Nature and the Social Order

The chief executive must carry the message both to those outside and to those inside the organization. Speeches provide the
opportunity to enlist people in your cause, to sell them on your program of change. How well you are able to do so depends on how
well you can deliver a speech. Most people will assume that if you
cannot tell them clearly what you stand for, you may not stand for
much. As chief executive, regardless of how small your organization—rather, especially if it is small—you should tactfully but
aggressively seek opportunities to speak to outside audiences. Let it
be known to local service clubs and other forums that you are available. Ask your board members to help find opportunities. Become
a better speaker and never pass up an opportunity.

The first step in bringing about change is to change people's
minds. They have to be persuaded, and that requires that they be
given pertinent information. The vision that the change represents,

and its advantages to them and to the institution, must be clearly communicated. Once a program of change is begun, staff need a continual supply of information in order to remain motivated and to implement the program successfully. Thus, the change-oriented chief executive has a vital interest in how well important information about the organization is communicated throughout.

Public Speaking

Most new chief executives have had little chance to practice public speaking. Previous positions usually did not require it, and the educational system has not been of much help; the contrast between the amount of attention given to writing in our schools and colleges, and that given to speaking, is ludicrous. But all is not lost: anyone intelligent enough to become a chief executive in the first place can learn to be a satisfactory speaker. Here is a program of self-improvement that works:

Begin by reading a few books on public speaking, such as *Standing Ovation* by James Humes (1988) and by viewing one or two instructional videotapes. Pay close attention to the style of good speakers and ask yourself what it is that makes them effective. Join the Toastmasters; you will learn a great deal about effective speaking and meet some new colleagues. Ask members of your senior staff who hear your speeches to provide you with constructive criticism. (You will need a thick skin and your staff will have to believe that you will not shoot the messenger.) With the technology available today, you have a great advantage over previous generations of speakers: you can see yourself as the audience sees you. If you are new at speech making, practice and have some trusted person (or yourself) videotape your practice sessions. If the organization to which you are speaking is making a video- or audiotape of your speech, make sure that you get a copy and study it. "Know thyself," however painful at first.

Prepare your speeches carefully. Begin by reviewing what you know about the invitation to speak: the nature and size of the audience, the size and shape of the room, the placement of the podium, the length of time you are expected to speak, your place in the schedule. If there are gaps in your information, get in touch as early as possible with the person who invited you. Learn why you were invited to speak to this particular audience and what message you are expected to give. (You do not always have to deliver that precise message, but you should at least know what it is and stray from it only for a good purpose.)

At larger organizations and at smaller ones where the executive is a reluctant speaker, it will be tempting and sometimes necessary to have someone else write your speeches. When you write your own speeches, however, they are your own creations, reflecting your thoughts and revealing more accurately what you believe and are trying to convey. Your speeches will be easier to remember and deliver; you will appear more relaxed and in command as you give them.

Try preparing your speeches from an outline. Several software programs make it easy to jot down ideas as they occur to you and then to rearrange them into a logical order. Keep at this process until you have a complete, though not word-for-word, outline. If the speech is not too formal, try to speak from your outline rather than from a complete text. You will be selecting your actual words as you speak, giving the speech a feeling of spontaneity and allowing you to deliver it more effectively. Most important of all, speaking from notes rather than a full text allows you to make better eye contact and prevents the temptation to read the speech, head down.

If the speech is to be delivered in a more formal setting, write it out in full and edit until it is as good as you can make it. (As Humes points out, no truly great speech was ever delivered from notes. One could also say that no great speech was ever delivered from overhead transparencies. Language worth remembering needs to be crafted.) As you write, constantly try to put yourself in the place of the audience. Understand where its members are apt to be in their thinking and where it is that you want to move them. Read sections and finally the whole out loud; this will help you to avoid longer sentences, which work better in writing where if necessary the reader can go back over the more difficult passages. In a speech, you have only one chance to get your message across and sentences need to be shorter and immediately clear. Ask a colleague to give the draft a critical edit.

The most critical aspect of public speaking is summed up by Humes: "Words must never leave your mouth while you are looking down at the text" (1988, p. 106). Looking up and directly out while you are in the act of speaking is the single most important factor in public speaking; without it, little else matters. Let me cite as evidence three of the greatest speakers of this century:

Martin Luther King, Jr. Perhaps the most famous American address of the latter half of this century was King's "I Have a Dream." Most of us have seen video clips of this great speech. How many times did Dr. King deliver his words while looking down at his text? The answer: not once! Either he had memorized what he wanted to say or a lifetime of speaking and preaching brought those memorable phrases to his lips. However he did it, his head was high and his eyes made continual contact with his audience. Would his words have been so moving had he read them, head down? Of course not. If you have a dream, you do not have to read it, you know it by heart!

John F. Kennedy. Many of us either saw President Kennedy's inaugural address on television at the time or have seen a video recording. Certainly all of us recall his most famous line, "Ask not what your country can do for you; ask what you can do for your country." If you can capture in your mind's eye his delivery of that line, you will recall that it came with JFK looking into the camera and out at his audience. (In fact, he jabbed his finger at them!) Imagine instead the impact if he had read that sentence and the rest of his speech, head buried in his text. Would that have stirred thousands to join the Peace Corps and a young Bill Clinton to a life of public service? (In his biography of JFK, Nigel Hamilton [1992] reports that early in Kennedy's political career he was a terrible speaker. But we remember him as one of the best, possibly the best, presidential speaker since World War II. He got lots of practice and he improved.)

Winston Churchill. Prime Minister Churchill had a mastery of language, written and spoken, that few have matched. His speeches were given over the radio or in the House of Commons long before the arrival of computers, television, and TelePrompTers. Few in this country ever saw Churchill speak, and a dwindling number remember hearing him on the radio. Yet many of his phrases will always live in memory and in books of quotations. Humes (1988) tells us that Churchill had his speeches typed in short phrases so that he could deliver them while making eye contact. He used the same technique as all good speakers.

None of us will ever match the level of oratory of King, JFK, and Churchill. Nevertheless, simply following Humes's advice about eye contact will make an adequate speaker out of almost anyone. But it will take practice. As he points out, when you first look down to read the next phrase, you will experience an uneasy sensation. You will have broken eye contact with your audience and will fear that you have lost them. But that is in your mind, not theirs. They are still there, digesting your last words, and your looking down will seem perfectly natural. Most will not even realize that you are doing so to retrieve your next phrase. If you have prepared properly, it will take only a second or two for you to absorb those next few words and to look up to deliver them. If you have outlined, written, and edited the speech yourself, and practiced delivering it, even though you do not have it memorized, its phrases will leap off the page and your tongue.

Practice this kind of delivery in front of a mirror before you give your next speech. Stand erect, have your text on a lectern or podium at a height and angle that makes it easy for you to look down and retrieve your next phrase. Force yourself not to say a single word unless you are looking into your own eyes in the mirror.

Try this a few times, and you will begin to receive a new level of compliment on your speeches. As you perfect this technique, your level of confidence will rise, and you can spend more time on content, knowing that your delivery will get your message across.

Be especially careful about how you begin a speech. The first and last sentences are the most important. Memorize the first few so that there is no risk of uttering them without making eye contact. If you can tell a joke well and if you know a good one, there is no reason not to begin that way in order to put your audience at ease. But get on with it—you are not a comedian.

Try not to speak for more than twenty to twenty-five minutes. If you cannot make your points in that amount of time, the topic is too complex and you would be well-advised to choose another.

You should not always take questions after you speak. In some settings they can be handled well, and we have all heard speakers who were more effective in the give-and-take than in their prepared remarks. In a more formal setting, however, your subsequent, off-the-cuff answers may well detract from the fine impression your carefully crafted words and delivery style have created.

Internal Communication

Effective communication within an organization makes sense both in principle and in practice. As a principle, people have a fundamental right to basic information about their workplace, particularly those aspects that have the greatest bearing on their performance and success. Speaking practically, the more employees know about their organization and how their jobs and those above and below them fit in, the more effectively they can perform. The more staff understand the institutional vision and the plan for achieving it, the more motivated they will be and the more of their effort will be directed toward these larger institutional aims. The more they know, the more they will be able to see the effect of their own performance on the institution as a whole and the more fulfillment they will take from their job. The more fulfillment, the better the performance, and so on.

Another overriding practical need exists for improved internal communication today. Every writer about the modern organization has noted that economies are changing so that what people know and what they can learn is more important than what they can make. As Drucker (1989) states, "The biggest shift—bigger by far than the changes in politics, government, or economics—is the shift to the knowledge society in all developed non-Communist countries. The social center of gravity has shifted to the knowledge worker" (p. 173). Or as Senge (1990) noted, learning disabilities are tragic in children, but they are fatal in organizations. Because of them, few corporations live even half as long as a person—most die before they reach the age of forty (pp. 17–18). The theme is the same in these and in countless other books: the modern organization, including those in the nonprofit sector, will depend on how much its workers know and how well knowledge is distributed throughout. At the very least, staff need to know how their own organization works.

To have an effective program of internal communication, staff must be made aware continually of the importance of sharing information and of learning from their colleagues, both formally and informally. The spirit, led visibly by the chief executive, is that no opportunity for informal communication will be missed. But such informal methods, while necessary, are not sufficient—more formal ones are required, as described below. For them, the chief executive must assign responsibility to a person or group, allocate the necessary budget, evaluate the success of the program, and play a prominent personal role in it. Here are some proven techniques:

Work-group presentations. Members of a unit—a department at a larger institution or the entire staff at a smaller one—can schedule weekly meetings, perhaps during lunch, at which individuals describe their work and how it fits within the organization. The chief executive can attend some and even be a presenter.

Management seminars. Staff members with a particular skill can conduct seminars for fellow staff members, who will not only learn the technique being described but also what their co-workers do well.

Written reports. The chief executive and other senior administrators should issue periodic reports to staff on important institutional matters. For example, the chief executive might issue a quarterly report with timely information about the organization. With the advantage of word processing, the chief executive can draft a single informational document and extract sections as the basis for one report tailored for the board and another aimed at staff.

Local area networks. At organizations with electronic mail networks, internal staff communications can be posted for all to read. Indeed, an electronic newsletter could be devised.

Newsletters and newspapers. The key to a successful program of internal communication is to make it not an option but a requirement—this is the curse and the blessing of a publication that is supposed to appear on a regular schedule. Those responsible know that the publication must appear on a certain date and that they must come up with enough copy to fill it. They cannot escape their responsibility merely by declaring that nothing worthy of communicating could be found. The existence of a scheduled publication thus produces a critical shift in mind-set: instead of waiting until the mood strikes or one is forced to communicate to avoid embarrassment, now the staff of the publication and senior management including the chief executive must regularly search for material worth including. It is surprising how much worthy information can found to communicate when one has to.

The mere existence of an internal staff newsletter sends the message that the organization and the chief executive believe in the importance of internal communication and that they are doing something about it. With desktop publishing, any institution can now produce an informative weekly or monthly staff newsletter easily and at low cost. If size warrants it, the newsletter can become a newspaper, though more staff and a larger budget will then be required. If staff come to see the internal newsletter merely as the mouthpiece of the chief executive, however, its credibility and usefulness will be undermined. Somehow, such an internal organ must find an independent voice, yet not work at cross-purposes to the chief executive's vision. This is difficult but can be done. Here is a case where at least the perception of independence was lost:

> A staff newspaper at a large museum was founded over the objections of those who thought it a poor use of scarce resources. It passed one kind of test when the chief executive retired and the successor arrived, eager to find policies to change and areas to cut so as to differentiate himself from his predecessor. As soon as he realized the utility of the newspaper in presenting himself and his activities in a favorable light, however, the paper was quickly removed from the list of planned excisions. As it came to be more of a mouthpiece for the chief executive, however, its credibility fell.

Speeches by the chief executive. The chief executive of a small nonprofit may have many occasions at which the whole staff is together and at which they can be told of the executive's vision and plan for the organization. The leaders of larger institutions should create occasions at which to address the entire staff in a "state of the institution" speech. This provides an opportunity to reinforce the vision and direction of the institution and to put your own stamp on it.

Communication to the chief executive. It is important that every staff member have a chance to observe and to hear from the chief executive in the way just described and, potentially at least, be able to ask the chief executive a question. Although the advice in the section above cautioned against taking questions after your speeches to those outside the organization, you must be willing to entertain questions after you speak to your staff. Answer honestly; if you do not know, say so and promise to find out.

The chief executive who is especially good at it may even wish to hold a question and answer session instead of a speech, following more the format of a presidential press conference than a state of the union address. After a few opening remarks, throw the floor open to questions, showing yourself willing to try to answer anything that is asked. But be sure that you have nothing to hide, otherwise you can end up as did this chief executive:

> A college president decided to show himself as more open than his predecessor and arranged to give a comprehensive speech to the faculty on the budget. At the end, flushed with success, he agreed to take questions. After a few perfunctory ones, a junior member asked hesitantly if the rumor were true that the president planned to reduce a key faculty benefit in the budget, expressing doubt that the allegation could be accurate since the president had not mentioned it during his exhaustive presentation. A dead silence fell, the president stammered and turned to the provost, who acknowledged that the rumor was indeed true. Cries of "bad faith" filled the air; the president was forced to resign a few months later; the provost was passed over for the presidency. The lesson? There are no secrets.

Sometimes unusual opportunities for communication come up; the astute chief executive will always be on the lookout for them. Here is a lesson from a librarian:

> The newly hired director of a library wanted to differentiate himself from his cool and aloof forerunner. He placed a large suggestion box near the front door where it was impossible to miss and accompanied it with a prominent sign saying that he would answer every question and post both the question and his answer within twenty-four hours. For the first few weeks, he worked an extra two to three hours every day keeping his promise. But keep it he did. Over time, as fewer questions remained unanswered, the task became less and less burdensome; morale and library usage shot up; he and his box became legend.

Instead of leaving communication to the discretion of individuals and their response to the exhortations of the chief executive, a plan could be prepared showing how internal communication is to be improved, based on elements like those described above plus others. This process will produce new ideas, underscore the importance of communication, and lodge responsibility for it with a few individuals.

10

· ·

Fundraising Strategies and Practice

*Philanthropy is almost the only virtue which is suffi-
ciently appreciated by mankind.*

Henry Thoreau, Walden

Without a successful program of fundraising, few nonprofit
organizations and few nonprofit chief executives can succeed. Fortunately, fundraising depends largely on careful planning,
a modicum of courage, and diligent follow-through. One can learn
how to do it, and many professional associations and organizations
offer workshops and training. The National Society of Fund-Raising
Executives and the Council for the Advancement and Support of
Education both have exemplary programs. *The President and Fund-
Raising,* edited by Fisher and Quehl (1989), is an excellent guide
from which all nonprofit chief executives can benefit. *Fund-Raising:
Principles and Practices* (Worth, 1993) is also a useful compendium.
Howe's *The Board Member's Guide to Fund Raising* (1991) has an
excellent step-by-step scenario for asking for a gift, adapted and
summarized here in Resource D.

Nonprofit organizations not only need to raise money, they must
maintain good relations with a wide set of individuals and groups,
from the disadvantaged to the well-to-do. Most of those outside—
community leaders, politicians, funders, and even trustees—expect
to deal directly with the chief executive, which is why 25 to 40 per-

cent of the time of a typical nonprofit chief executive is spent on external affairs. When a major fund drive is underway, the percentage is higher. This work is vital to the long-term health of the organization, yet for several reasons spending so much time on fundraising and external affairs may prove difficult. For one thing, the typical new chief executive has less experience with external affairs than with any other part of the new portfolio. For another, most people feel uncomfortable asking someone else for money; indeed, we are strongly socialized against it. Mark Twain advised, "Friendship . . . will last through a whole lifetime, if not asked to lend money" (1964, p. 59). To ask a near stranger for money, even though it is not for one's personal benefit, requires that lifelong habits be overcome. Some people are never able to do so.

Too, the chief executive is always confronted with urgent (but often low-payoff) internal tasks that need immediate attention. It is tempting, and often satisfying in the short run, to stay at one's desk and to postpone external matters. Instead, delegate those low-payoff tasks to others and get out where the money is to be found.

The elemental fact of fundraising is that most of those who have money must and will give some of it away. They expect to be asked and the chief executive can only be faulted for not asking. As explained below, it is only when you ask for a donation from an individual that a direct, personal appeal is made; other requests are to agency and foundation program officers, who are fellow professionals.

> Private foundations are required by law to give away a percentage of their assets each year; that they will is a certainty. The only uncertainty is, who will present them with the most persuasive case?

> Government agencies annually convince Congress and the Office of Management and Budget to fund their grant programs. A program that receives too few applications and is unable to expend its funds is apt to lose them the following

year to another office or agency. Neither the program officer nor the agency head wants that to happen and therefore agencies attempt to grant all of the money that they have set aside in a particular program.

A corporate foundation is in the same position as a government agency: its director has persuaded the chief executive and board to set aside a sum of money for some worthy philanthropic program. If that money cannot be expended, the director appears inept and the money is apt to be withdrawn.

The tax laws make it advantageous (though less so than previously) for wealthy individuals to make donations and many do. They are prepared to give to the worthy charity that approaches them in the appropriate way and that makes the most persuasive case. The wealthier the prospect, the more they expect to be asked. But the request should be made only after careful cultivation, when the time is right. The prospective donor will know that you ask not for yourself but for a mission in which you believe deeply and that you would be derelict were you not to ask.

In summary, given the need of donors to give, and the importance of your cause, you have nothing to fear: go ahead and ask.

The Fundraising Program

Beyond its direct monetary rewards, fundraising has several other benefits. First, the process of raising money in a competitive environment requires that an organization understand and then communicate its special attributes. To succeed at fundraising, a nonprofit must have a mission statement, a strategic plan, a balanced budget, and people who can represent the institution effectively. These are necessary ingredients of institutional success in any case. Second, in the process of fundraising, the chief executive and other representatives are out and about in the community, meeting people of means, gauging their interest in the institution, and recruiting volunteers for various institutional activities. Individuals begin to sort themselves out by their degree of commitment and willingness to work. Those who show the most interest are excellent candidates for board membership. Third, success at raising money becomes a gauge by which people judge an institution—one that is highly effective becomes respected and sought after; the more it raises, the more people want to be associated with it and the more it is then able to raise. Conversely, an institution with a poor reputation at fundraising becomes suspect: it may have no message, poor leadership, or both. Donors will look elsewhere.

The ingredients of a successful fundraising program are as follows:

- A succinct, appropriate, and persuasive mission statement.

- The ability to communicate what is special about the institution and its mission.

- Sufficient resources—staff, materials, volunteers, time from the chief executive and board, and access to information and technology—to accomplish the task.

- An institution with a positive image in the community. Any image, unless it is strongly negative, is better than none. But a new chief executive who inherits an organization about which many feel negative must reverse that view before any significant amount of money can be raised.

- Ideally, a tradition of fundraising success. If you are not so fortunate as to inherit an institution with such a record, make sure that you leave your successor with a stronger tradition than you found.

Medium-sized and larger nonprofits have at least one person beyond the chief executive whose major responsibility is fundraising. Many smaller organizations do not, and the chief executive is a jack- or jill-of-all-trades. Ultimately, without a professional development executive, an institution will be handicapped. Not every institution will be able to have such a person, but most should aspire and work toward it. Howe (1991) suggests that an organization with an annual budget of $300,000 should have at least one person spending half time on development; those with budgets of $500,000 and up should have at least one spending full time. Where such allocations of personnel are simply not possible, maximum benefit has to be derived from board participation in fundraising.

For those organizations that are large enough to have a development staff, it is critical that ambitious but achievable goals be set and that performance be evaluated. Here is a case where the chief development officer declined to set goals for his own program, requiring the chief executive to do so:

> A new chief executive met with the head of the development depart-
> ment and inquired as to the unrestricted giving target for the following
> year. The development officer replied smoothly, "Mr. President, we do
> not have targets here; we just raise all the money we can." The pres-
> ident replied, "Oh, but now you do and it is 125 percent of this year's
> figure." The development officer blanched; the target was not only
> met but exceeded.

Turning a lagging development program around may take three years. Make sure that you and your board leaders understand this and do not expect results too quickly. Fundraising must be thought of as a Program with a capital P, ideally one that was going on well before the current chief executive arrived and that will go on far into the future. An institution that approaches raising money opportunistically—rushing out after first one potential gift and then another without adequate preparation and no plan or strategy—may have some limited success, but its effort will falter as soon as those who have used this technique leave. Better to develop a dependable program that generates growing amounts year by year.

Individual Donors

Foundations and government agencies are notoriously fickle; just when a grant program seems to have achieved maturity and to have become effective, the foundation has a staff or board turnover and the program is scrapped in favor of a new one. Whatever the program, competition among nonprofits for grants is fierce. This line of thought leads to the realization that individuals who have some particular connection to the institution, perhaps through being on the board, are the most likely source of funds. This is especially true for the all-important unrestricted funds—those that pay the light bill and your salary. Almost all grants from foundations and agencies are of the restricted variety. You receive a dollar, but you spend it on some worthy program. Often the grant does not carry an overhead reimbursement, so that the program, however worthy, is a net drain on resources. In fact, some 85 percent of all gifts to nonprofits come from individuals.

The fundraising program for individuals begins with the identification of potential donors, proceeds through establishing and enhancing their interest and involvement, goes on to major giving, and ends with a bequest. Every now and then, a major donor will appear suddenly, but most donors reach the major gift stage only after passing through the beginning and intermediate stages.

The new chief executive may find that current trustees have recently been asked to make what for each of them is a major gift. They will need a rest and time to develop a relationship with the new executive. Meanwhile, other prospects can be discovered and cultivated. The names of potential new donors can be suggested by trustees and friends and uncovered through research. It is remarkable, if not a little frightening, what can be learned about individuals from public sources of information. For example, for a fee a nonprofit can have a computer screening done, which will iden-

tify—from public information about zip code, automobile registra-
tion, credit history, and so forth—all of the nonprofit's members
who live in a certain area and who are predicted to have a specified
level of wealth. This technique should be used with great caution
lest the organization appear to be invading a donor's privacy.

Once a new prospect is identified, you can find a way through a
trustee or friend of the institution to make an approach. For example, a trustee can invite the potential donor to have lunch with the
new chief executive. If the prospect repeatedly avoids the invitation, move on to another. If the individual is not apt to be a major
donor, the development officer or another member of the staff can
make the contact and initiate the process. Individual donors and
board members expect and need to be treated as individuals.
Prospects for large gifts require almost constant special treatment—
to go too far will prove difficult (Howe, 1991). A special program
of cultivation should be established for each major donor, with an
appropriate timetable.

Most wealthy people are used to making decisions and understand that they are being cultivated. At the right moment, perhaps
after six months or a year for the largest donors, the stage will be
set. Then follow this simple rule: *ask for the money!* Leave no doubt
in the donor's mind that you have asked and for what amount. Talk
to any experienced fundraiser and you will hear stories of chief executives who, when the time finally came, simply could not ask for
the gift. They got to the point of consummation but then were
unable to make the request or managed to ask but left the amount
unspecified. Since few give more than asked, this is a sure way to go
home empty-handed or with a gift well below the donor's potential.
It is also a sure way to lose a good development officer, who does
not want to see hard preparation wasted, as in this case:

> One chief executive was exceptionally adept at impressing trustees
> and other friends of the institution. Unfortunately, he had never grown
> comfortable with the need to ask for donations. Time after time, his
> development officer would set up a meeting with a prospective donor,

only to have the chief executive either cancel or show up but make small talk instead of a request for a gift. Finally, the development officer learned that she had to accompany and prod her boss or no gift of appropriate size would ever get made. The institution raised much less than its potential.

I can sum up this section in no better way than by quoting Howe, who offers six cardinal rules of philanthropy (1991, pp. 6–8). The chief executive who can turn these principles into a program of fundraising, and who puts them into practice daily, is bound to succeed.

- People give money because they want to.
- People do not give unless they are asked.
- People give money to people.
- People give money to opportunities, not to needs.
- People give to success, not to distress.
- People give money to make a change for the good.

One of Howe's points is so fundamental that it bears more attention than a single bullet: donors give not from pity but from pride. They want those in their circle to compliment their wisdom in associating themselves with such a worthy and important cause. When they tell their friends that they have made a major gift to your institution, they want to see respect, not bafflement at how good money could be thrown after bad. Donors want to give to winners, not to ward off failure, since experience has shown that the salvation will be only temporary, as in this case:

A theater that had fallen upon hard times made a last-ditch appeal to which many responded generously. Two years later, the hard times had returned. Now, however, most donors felt "once burnt, twice

shy" and declined further support, forcing the theater to close. Had
the donors insisted the first time around on management changes
and a long-range plan, the theater would have shrunk but might have
survived.

An important duty of the chief executive is to instill a sense of
pride in the institution: the chief executive personally must be visibly proud and cause that feeling to become contagious. The person
who said, "I would be pessimistic, but it probably wouldn't work"
was right—it does not. Be blatantly optimistic, especially when in
the presence of donors.

Foundations

One advantage of dealing with private and government foundations
is that they typically put out annual reports describing their programs and listing their previous grants. Many issue requests-for-
proposals that explain their interests and procedures. Program
officers expect to meet with representatives of nonprofits who want
to learn more about their programs. Just be sure that you do not use
up too much of their time. The key to receiving a grant for your
organization is to show how it would foster your mission and that
of the foundation.

To receive such a grant and to make the work it outlines worth
doing in the first place, the project and the proposal describing it
must have intellectual substance. After you have ensured that proposals emanating from your institution have such content, the task
then becomes to present it in the most persuasive and appealing way.

Here are a few guidelines:

Delegate responsibility. If your organization is large enough,
assign finished proposals to an expert proposal writer. Depending on size, the writer may work full or part time at that task
or be hired as a contractor. A good proposal writer will under-

stand both your organization and the foundation and how to make their needs mesh. Develop a standard procedure for the preparation and submission of proposals and delegate to the writer the full authority of the chief executive to insist that all deadlines be met.

Train staff. One of your staff can become an expert in desktop publishing, so you can send the final draft of the proposal to that person. Make sure that each proposal emanating from your organization is consistent in style and is not only perfect but elegant.

Follow the rules. Each step of the request-for-proposal is important. If the grantor requires that six items be covered in the proposal, cover six, not five or seven, and in the same order. If the maximum number of pages to be submitted is fifteen, never have more and try to have one or two less. (Think what a pleasant surprise this will be for the panel who one day must review thirty-five proposals!) Arrange to submit a preliminary proposal to the agency or foundation so that you can use their advice to improve the final version.

Take responsibility. Except at the largest institutions, review and sign every proposal yourself. Be rigorous in your appraisal. If you are at a larger institution, review proposals yourself periodically—it will keep you informed and your staff on their toes. Find ways to improve the proposal (but make sure that you send it back within the deadline schedule). Reject proposals that do not meet the institution's guidelines; the message that they must be met will quickly be perceived. Require that the finance department review and formally approve each proposal.

Follow through. When a proposal is turned down, find out why. Government agencies, which operate in the sunshine, must tell you, and private foundations often will.

As noted above, foundations are increasingly disinclined to make grants for operations and it is increasingly difficult to obtain reimbursement for overhead costs. In effect, some foundations encourage nonprofits to take on worthy projects, ones in which the foundation has declared its own interest, but then deny them reimbursement for the full cost of the program. What does it mean for an institution that has, say, a negotiated overhead recovery rate of 20 percent to be denied that rate on a grant of $50,000? It means that the institution must take $10,000 from its precious sources of unrestricted revenue and apply it to the grant. The world may be a better place because the work was done, but the institution is $10,000 in the hole. Eventually, a point of diminished returns is reached at which the cost is greater than the institution can afford: while doing more and better projects, but with less overhead recovery, it is slowly going broke (Howe, 1991). This is a larger issue than any one nonprofit can solve. But it ought to receive attention from the boards of private and corporate foundations.

Planned Giving

This term refers to a gift that comes through an estate or via one of the several charitable trusts, in which donors transfer assets now in return, for example, for lifetime income from the principal. Few small institutions have adequate planned giving programs and many larger ones do not. Some, however, such as Pomona College, have been spectacularly successful over decades. Organizations have been slow to establish planned giving programs that involve estates for several reasons. A planned giving program requires hard and sustained work over a long period, and often the effort fails with a particular individual. It is awkward to discuss a person's death with that person, especially where money is at issue; not many development staffers can do it well. (It is not true that a donor who makes a deferred gift to your institution thereby prolongs life expectancy by a full decade!) Planned giving requires technical expertise on tax and estate law. The payoff is in the future, after the donor has departed this vale of tears and usually after today's fundraisers have left the organization; someone else will get the credit.

None of these is a good reason for failing to explore this important future source of funds. Chief executives are supposed to be thinking long run, attempting to leave the organization better than they found it. The technical expertise can pay for itself over time, and the expense could be shared by several nonprofits (Howe, 1991). Elderly, wealthy individuals are already planning their estates or should be; there is nothing embarrassing about discussing their plans with them as long as it is done tactfully.

Community Visibility and Entertainment

The chief executive will need to spend time at community and social events—receptions, parties, banquets—where contacts can be made and the flag waved. Depending on the community, the chief executive may want to join a local service club such as Rotary (which now admits women). If you represent a large institution, however, it may be better to follow the advice of Fisher (1984) and to address such clubs rather than to belong to them—membership produces obligations that you may not wish to fulfill.

Many institutions will expect the chief executive to join a private club and will pay the dues. These can be useful in getting to know the community and to be seen as part of it. But be careful: some private clubs have a history of discrimination against all but WASP males. Generally they are now open to all, but double-check before joining. Nonprofits should not support organizations that discriminate on the basis of sex, race, or religion. Here is an example of a club that belatedly, but finally, did the right thing:

The Collegiate Club had been restricted to males since its founding. Its halls were lined with banners, pendants, plaques, coats-of-arms, and the like from colleges and universities across the country. In response to a threat from a city councilwoman to introduce legisla-

tion banning single-sex private clubs, the club held an open debate
on the matter. The male president of a local college attended and
brought along a female guest. He asked how, since all the colleges
in the area were coeducational, and since many institutions in other
parts of the country now had female presidents, the club could
restrict membership to males *and* go on calling itself the Collegiate
Club? Various members offered a defense but fell silent when the
president introduced his guest: a woman who had just been selected
as the next president of the university located only a few blocks from
the club! The issue was quickly decided in favor of admitting women.

A new chief executive may be invited to serve on the board of
another nonprofit, which is a good idea as long as no conflict exists.
Service on the board of a for-profit company can help the chief
executive to be better known in the business community, to learn
more about business from the inside, and to develop a closer relationship with a trustee. Since for-profit boards provide a fee for their
directors, serving on one can be a significant supplement to salary.
But it can also be, and has been, overdone by nonprofit executives
who sit on too many outside boards.

Some nonprofit chief executives, especially those at the larger
institutions, need to entertain. Academic presidents often live in a
university-owned house and are expected to host numerous events
(Resource B offers some additional factors to consider regarding
institutional housing). Most chief executives enjoy entertaining,
although everyone has a limit. If you are at an institution where
some or much entertainment goes with the position, here are some
suggestions for maximizing the enjoyment:

Develop a style. The way you entertain should express your per-
sonality and that of your institution (and spouse if you have
one). Think about the purpose of each event in advance;
otherwise, you may fail to make the personal contact that the
event is designed to produce.

Have it catered. Since your entertainment is on behalf of your institution and not yourself, the organization should pay for it. Thus, wherever an event takes place, hire a caterer at the expense of the organization. Your spouse, if any, should be able to choose how involved to be in the planning of the event.

Train the caterer. If you entertain in your home, you should be able to arrive five minutes before the event and have everything be just the way you like it. To reach this point will take some trial and error.

Set up a schedule. It is up to you to decide on a routine that suits you for each kind of event that takes place in your home. For example, have your dinner parties begin at, say, 6:30 P.M. and end at 10:00 P.M., at which time rise, say a few words of thanks, and remain standing. Your guests will be thankful for a good night's sleep and that they did not have to appear ungrateful by being the first to leave. Keep in mind Homer's admonition: "Treat a guest well as long as he is in the house and speed him when he wants to leave it" (1952, p. 266).

Finally, be careful how institutional funds are spent; many a chief executive has gotten into trouble because of extravagant spending on entertainment or accoutrements.

Working with Your Board

The management of a balance of power is a permanent undertaking.

Henry Kissinger, White House Years

To many who work at nonprofit organizations, the trustees, or directors, are seldom seen, showing up for a meeting and then disappearing until the next. Many new chief executives will not have worked closely with these visitors and may not be fully aware of their importance or how to interact with them. But the board is both the legal embodiment of the institution and the chief executive's key constituency:

- The board holds the organization in trust and is legally obligated to see that it survives in good health while fulfilling its mission or adopting another. In extreme cases, the board may be required to close an institution. Legally, the board *is* the institution.

- In almost every instance, the board will have been chartered at or before the very founding of the organization: no group can claim greater continuity and longevity. The board perpetuates mission and history.

195

- If the board will not support the major policy initiatives of the chief executive, they cannot be adopted. Without the board, you cannot be an agent of change.

- As noted below, a primary responsibility of the board is to select, evaluate, and when necessary dismiss the chief executive. The chief executive is formally answerable to the board and to no other group.

It will prove difficult to pay too much attention to your board.

Role of the Board

Boards in specific sectors of the nonprofit world have their own organizations: the Association of Governing Boards of Universities and Colleges and the Museum Trustees Association, to name two. The AGB has issued many useful publications on trusteeship that have application beyond academic boards. The National Center for Nonprofit Boards has an excellent set of programs and publications that are particularly appropriate for smaller organizations. One chief executive, however, hoped to keep the news of the existence of such organizations a deep secret:

A new chief executive asked the chair how familiar the board was with the programs of the national association of trustees. To his surprise, he learned that the chair and other senior board members had never heard of it. Further discreet inquiries revealed that the predecessor had carefully kept the existence of the association hidden from the board, apparently in the belief that better board practices would reduce his ability to control: their ignorance would be his bliss.

Fisher (1991, p. 92) has adapted the list of responsibilities of governing boards as defined by the AGB, as follows:

1. To appoint the president
2. To evaluate the institution
3. To assess board policies
4. To support the president
5. To review the performance of the president
6. To renew the mission
7. To approve the long-range plans
8. To oversee the programs
9. To ensure financial solvency
10. To preserve organizational independence
11. To represent both the institution and the public
12. To serve as a court of appeal
13. To determine board performance

As these duties generally reflect, the board is responsible for policy while its implementation is to be reserved for the chief executive and the staff. The board sets the overall direction for the organization; the chief executive serves as the board's agent, trying to walk the tightrope (not sit on the fence) between administration and policy and acting as an interpreter between the board and the staff. O'Connell (1993) takes a contrary point of view, however: "The worst illusion ever perpetrated . . . is that the board of directors makes policy and the staff carries it out. The board, with the help of staff, makes policy, and the board, with the help of staff, carries it out" (p. 46). These apparently opposite positions are hard to reconcile, though the argument is complicated because the AGB and Fisher are describing academic governance, where the faculty constitute a third house in addition to the board and the administration. O'Connell, on the other hand, is addressing the nonacademic nonprofits that have no faculty, that are generally smaller, and in which the board typically is more directly involved.

Having served as chief executive of five nonprofit institutions (two large museums and three colleges), and having been a member of many boards, my experience leads me to come down firmly on the side of separating policy and administration to the extent possible. History tells us unequivocally that if the abuse of power is to be avoided, a system of checks and balances is necessary—absolute power corrupts absolutely. When the line between administration and policy becomes blurred or disappears, checks and balances likewise disappear and one individual or group can both set policy and implement it. In good times, or where minor matters are concerned, this may do no harm, but on major institutional decisions, or in a time of crisis, it can invite disaster.

Whatever the size and nature of the institution, the respective roles of the board, the chief executive, and the staff must be clear both in governance documents and in practice. Certain tasks must be assigned to the executive and the staff, everyone should know what those tasks are, and the board should stay out of them and evaluate the effectiveness with which they are accomplished. It is true that at the smallest nonprofits, some functions that would be performed by staff at large ones are carried out by trustee volunteers, thus blurring the line between policy and administration. While remaining grateful for their time and service, the chief executive should be on the alert to retain those matters that are indispensable for leadership.

Role of the Chief Executive

The role of the nonprofit chief executive vis-à-vis the board is, to say the least, complex. The board hires the executive, who then sometimes is made an ex officio member of the board. To be a member of a group that has the power to fire you is disconcerting. The board has almost all the statutory authority and legal power, yet its members are volunteers whose information comes primarily from the executive. Unless this complicated relationship is managed well, neither the board, the chief executive, nor the organization will succeed.

Given that the board hires and fires, it would seem logical for the chief executive always to defer to the board, acting perhaps in the role of clerk and facilitator. But when one considers that the board is a group of busy volunteers with the board chair often busier than most, one can see that if the executive is deferential, no one may lead. It is a misguided board chair who believes that the organization can truly be led by a part-time volunteer with little expertise in the mission of the organization or time to devote to it: nonprofits need both the chief executive and the volunteer board chair.

For this reason, a growing body of literature, added to and well summarized by Herman and Heimovics (1991, p. xiii), establishes that if "a nonprofit organization is to be effective, it is usually the chief executive who must engage the board in clarifying their respective and mutually-shared roles and responsibilities. . . . The chief executive is the center of leadership for the organization." Thus, the chief executive should find a way, unobtrusively but effectively, not only to lead the organization but to lead the board to a stronger and more rewarding performance. Drucker put it this way: "It is the CEO's responsibility to define the tasks of each, the board's and his or her own" (Jul.–Aug. 1989, p. 91).

Executive leadership of the board may be particularly hard to put into practice at the smaller nonprofits. There, as noted, board members and particularly the chair are apt to be more involved in administration and more likely to believe that they could run the organization as well as anyone. In such cases, it will take a great deal of tact and patience and sometimes the arrival of a new chair to put the executive in a position to provide the leadership that any board needs. But every nonprofit executive ought to strive to find ways of leading both the organization and the board. To put it bluntly, seldom will a board that fails blame itself—the chief executive will provide a ready scapegoat. To look out for your own self-interest and to be professional, you must take responsibility for the success of the board.

A principal responsibility of the chief executive is to keep the board and especially the chair adequately informed on all significant matters. The words *adequately* and *significant* are chosen advisedly. The board does not need to be told everything nor does it have time to hear it. The chief executive should tell the chair and where appropriate the rest of the board just a bit more than enough on all matters that may rise to the policy level. When in doubt, err on the side of disclosure. That way you will never surprise the board on an important matter. To err in this respect is to court dismissal or at least a loss of confidence, which will sooner or later lead to dismissal, as happened to this executive:

> The new chief executive of a medium-sized museum desperately wished to hire as deputy director a person who was driving a hard bargain. Against his better judgment and without consulting the board chair, he promised this candidate a special benefits package, one that turned out to violate the institution's policies. He was forced to retract the package, causing both the candidate and the board to lose confidence in him.

It should be unnecessary to say that above all, a chief executive should never under any circumstances lie. If it has come to the point where you cannot tell the board the truth and continue in office, resign. In any case, there are no secrets.

Realize that you and your organization necessarily occupy only a small part of the attention of most board members. Therefore, as the saying goes, "Tell them what you are going to tell them; tell them; then tell them what you told them." Even then, you may have to tell them at the next meeting what you told them at the last one. Be patient. Try to keep the line between policy and administration straight in your own mind and in theirs—and in the minds of your senior staff, as this example demonstrates:

> Well-meaning board members frequently dropped by the offices of a social service agency. Naturally, their conversations with staff often

turned to agency business. Occasionally, these discussions made their way to a board meeting, catching the executive and the board chair by surprise. The executive and the chair drafted a policy that board members were not to discuss business matters with staff without the knowledge and approval of the executive director.

Trustees want a chief executive whom they can respect and admire, even hold slightly in awe. To them, you are like a minister or rabbi: they expect you to be a paragon of virtue. They know that the church or synagogue depends on charity and that you are going to ask them for a donation. As long as you are careful, and do not prevail too much on any one trustee, you will be faulted only for not asking for their financial support.

Some new executives find themselves being entertained in opulent surroundings. Be careful: this can go to your head. Remember that it is not you the individual but you the chief executive who is being entertained and that trustee financial resources vastly exceed yours; do not even think about playing on their field. They do not expect it and you cannot afford it. Do not spend your own money on trustee entertainment; that is an obligation of your job, not a personal one, and your organization should pay for it.

The Chief Executive and the Chair

The chief executive's relationship with the chair should be more personal and open than with any other board member. While it may not be wise to become intimate friends, the chair does need to know you and to understand the major problems that confront you. The chair will realize that things are not going as smoothly as your public face would imply. Make the chair aware of what is going on behind the scenes and behind the board agenda, so that you can receive informed support when you need it. If the chair learns of important matters from others or has reason to doubt your veracity, you will have become part of the problem.

The practical reality is that the chair is the single most important person in determining your professional future. Although a compensation committee may have been established, other board members will have tacitly delegated to the chair responsibility for the evaluation, compensation, and retention of the chief executive. If the chair says you should be replaced, given his or her more intimate knowledge and the group dynamics of boards, you will be. If the chair thinks you are doing a fine job, you will get a raise.

One aspect of reporting to a board chair will require some getting used to: for the first time in your career, your work will not be overseen on a daily basis (Gilmore, 1988). To anyone observing you day in and day out, it would appear that you have no boss, that you are your own. But that is a dangerous illusion: you do have a boss and in some ways you have the least job security you have ever had, protected by fewer rules and more subject to the whim of one person. Chances are also that your boss is at least as busy as you are, having only fleeting moments to devote to the organization that you both serve. It will be largely up to you to ensure that the board chair is kept well informed on important matters yet not required to spend extensive amounts of time on briefings and meetings. A key indicator of your relationship and the importance the chair attaches to the post is how long it takes for the chair to return your telephone calls.

Three tips for dealing with the chair:

1. The chair of a board gave a new chief executive this advice: "Be yourself; that's who we hired." This told the chief executive not to try to emulate his predecessor and not to tailor his views to what he thought the board chair wanted to hear. The board had hired the chief executive because of qualities that he possessed and that they thought matched their need; they wanted him to give rein to those qualities. In any case, a phony is quickly spotted and replaced.

2. Recognizing how dependent you are on the chair can strike fear into the heart of even the most confident chief executive. At its worst, this can lead to fawning and obsequiousness. But as Fisher

(1991) points out, such attitudes are demeaning and ultimately self-defeating. Board chairs tend to be successful people, often chief executives who themselves report to boards; they will respect you for having your own views and stating them forcefully.

3. As Drucker (1986, p. 16) suggests, ask your board chair periodically, "What do I do to help you or hamper you?" This will show the chair that you understand your separate roles, that you want both of you and the organization to succeed, and that success will only come if you are a team.

The greatest risk comes on matters of major policy. Here the chair and the chief executive must be in sincere agreement. If the chair wants to take the organization down a different path than you would choose, you need to decide whether in good conscience you can bend on the point or whether to do so would violate essential principles. Do not pretend, even to yourself, because no chief executive can successfully promote an institution in whose major policies the executive does not truly believe. Better to resign than to compromise a deeply held principle, especially since staying on would not work in any case. Of course, it is far better to resolve conflicts well in advance so that resignation on principle never has to be considered.

If the chief executive is to provide leadership to the board, it follows that when the time comes to select a new board chair, the executive ought to have a prominent role and ideally an implicit veto power. This makes practical sense from the organization's point of view, because fulfillment of the mission clearly will be hampered if the chief executive and chair cannot work well together. Certainly the wise chief executive will want a strong voice in the selection of the person who, more than any other, determines the executive's future at the institution. It will prove more difficult for the executive of a smaller nonprofit to have a strong voice in the selection of the board chair, but it is an objective for which to strive. Even though you may not be able to accomplish it fully, you will pave the way for your successor.

Board Meetings

You will spend much time with the chair of your board, but other members will see you almost exclusively at board meetings. Given that the board is your most important constituency, and that most trustees observe you only in these meetings, your success and your job depend on them. If you have followed the advice of earlier chapters, you take every meeting seriously and prepare carefully, but especially when the meeting is of the board or its committees. Do not become overconfident, as this chief executive did:

> The president of a prestigious college decided to accept an offer to become the head of a historical society. He was quite confident, given his impressive credentials, that he could bluff his way through trustee meetings with little preparation. What he did not know until too late was that his predecessor had been highly organized and an excellent speaker, one who made her board meetings models of style and efficiency. He failed to prepare well, causing the board to doubt his abilities from their first meeting together. He was never able to recover their confidence.

At larger institutions, responsibility for staffing certain board committees—finance, education, development—should be delegated to the appropriate staff vice president. Make sure that before a board committee meeting you meet with the appropriate staff vice president to go over the agenda and any papers that will be handed out. You—not just the vice president—should understand everything that is to take place at the committee meeting and be able to answer any question except the most arcane. Your goal is never to be surprised and to appear leaderly. You have delegated, yes, but you retain knowledge and ultimate authority. If done well, the effectiveness with which your senior staff provide assistance to board committees can enhance their stature and yours.

Your staff do need to understand, however, that you are not equals, especially not at meetings with members of the board. In such a setting, the chief executive is always being evaluated, and by the very group that has the power to reward or discharge. Thus, vice presidents should never argue with nor compromise the chief executive in the presence of trustees—they may lose confidence in both of you. First, however, they may suggest privately that the chief executive replace the tactless staff member. Therefore, when a staff member needs to correct the chief executive, and conversely, it is best done outside the meeting.

Before each full board meeting, the chief executive and selected staff should meet with the chair to go over the agenda. The chief executive should send out in advance a written report, recording the important data and information for trustees. At each meeting, the chief executive should open with a hard-hitting oral statement that goes beyond the written report. Tell the trustees of successes and level with them about problems, but especially find ways to engage their minds and their voices. Once a year, give a truly presidential speech to the board. Standing erect, tell them of your vision. Convey that you understand the organization better than anyone and that you have a compelling and achievable dream for its future.

Remember that most trustees deal with numbers and personnel matters in their regular work and are on your board in hope of serving some higher cause. Take them beyond numbers and engage them in the mission. Help them to find ways of discovering joy in their work as trustees. Acquaint them with the real people that the organization is serving, so that their work is not merely impersonal and abstract. Once every year or two, take the board on a retreat off-site. Start the program late in the afternoon, stay overnight, and conclude the next afternoon. The retreat sessions should be informative but enjoyable, allowing trustees to get to know each other.

It is unfortunate but true that in most cases, and especially at large boards, confidentiality cannot be assumed. One board adjourned its meetings at noon on Saturday; by Monday confidential information from the meeting was known by certain staff confidantes of board members and returned to the chief executive, often altered as in the parlor game Gossip. All the more reason why the chief executive should have a completely confidential, open relationship with the board chair and perhaps with a small executive committee.

Finally, as Fisher (1984) suggests, as a courtesy to board members who may have matters that they prefer not to bring up in front of staff, schedule an executive session at the end of each board meeting. If such a session turns out to be needed, the time is available; if it is not needed, the meeting can adjourn early.

Strengthening the Board

Given its importance, over the long run no institution can be better than its board. Thus, one of the principal responsibilities of the board and the chief executive is to strengthen both the membership of the board and its operations. Few board members, however, have enough time to put into this important task; therefore, much of the responsibility will fall to the chief executive. This section provides some pointers for strengthening the operation of the board.

Since building up the board takes time, a short-term chief executive cannot do it. If you wish to leave a board considerably stronger than the one you found, you must have a sufficiently long tenure. To transform a board, that is, to replace many of the members you inherited, requires a strong, sympathetic chair and a tenure of six to eight years or more. Since boards in effect are clubs of volunteers, members naturally are reluctant to ask another to step down before the term has expired. Thus, to gain strength and giving potential, many boards have simply grown larger. This can be self-defeating— the more effective members tend to grow tired of dealing with the others and meetings become so large and unwieldy that little can be done. Usually, an executive committee is formed in response. If it takes over too much of the real business, however, members who are not on the executive committee can become offended or bored.

Therefore, one goal should be to get the size of the board down to the smallest effective number. Many institutions have three levels of boardlike activity: an executive committee, the board itself, and an advisory committee without statutory powers that provides advice and financial support as well as serving as a proving ground for prospective trustees. This tripartite organization is not easy to manage but if handled well can be effective.

Board members should be elected for multiyear terms that are renewable two or three times, after which a hiatus of a year should be mandatory. During that year, the poor performer can be let down gently and not invited to serve again; the superb trustee can be cultivated, kept involved (perhaps by being retained as a member of an important committee), and at the appropriate time, reelected. Many boards have mandatory retirement at a certain age. One chief executive, however, after serving with a board where the three key financial supporters were all over seventy, came to doubt the wisdom of an ironclad retirement rule. It may be better to put up with some deadwood than to force off those who have served the longest and who may provide much of the support. However, this is admittedly a matter of judgment. It should be understood in advance that a member who misses a specified number of meetings of the full board in succession—perhaps all that were scheduled within a single year—will be regarded as having resigned de facto. Here is an example in which the transition to a stronger board was well managed:

A young social service agency retained several dedicated board members who had been on the board since its founding and who had been instrumental in its growth. As the agency grew larger and more mature, however, it needed board members who could "give or get" funds and who were more skilled in dealing with larger and more complex organizations. The board chair skillfully persuaded these senior members to become "honorary life trustees," making them feel appreciated and opening up new slots on the board.

Finally, no person should be considered for membership on a board unless the chief executive explicitly concurs. If possible, the executive should meet privately with a candidate before an offer is extended. This ensures that the prospect will support the chief executive's agenda and reinforces the idea that the executive is the critical person at the organization. The board chair should then meet the candidate jointly with the chief executive. If the chief executive, rather than the board chair, extends the invitation, the executive's influence is enhanced.

Although the chief executive may have to take the lead in building the board, it obviously cannot be done without the direct assistance of trustees. Key to obtaining this assistance is the creation of a forum in which the condition and functioning of the board can be raised confidentially and in which the profile and performance of the board as a whole can be assessed. To provide this venue, each board needs a committee on trusteeship, or governance (Howe, 1991). Many boards have a committee on nominations; the work of that committee can be expanded to include these larger duties. The new committee, however titled, is responsible for the overall performance of the board. As Drucker (Jul.–Aug. 1989, p. 91) put it, "The key to making a board effective is to organize its work, not talk about its function."

A committee on trusteeship can take up the following sorts of questions, most of which could not be dealt with tactfully or efficiently in front of the entire board:

- Does the board have a clear statement that describes its duties and responsibilities? If not, many of the advantages that flow from a discussion of the organization's mission statement can derive from a board discussion of its own particular mission. Does the board have a clear statement on conflict of interest? (Model statements are available from the AGB and elsewhere.) Does the board receive the information that it needs far enough in advance of meetings?

- Does each board committee have a charge and is each well staffed and chaired?

- Are committees well led and well attended?

- Do members know each other? If not, a retreat may be in order.

- What do the members themselves think about the board's performance? Do they believe that the board meets too often or not often enough? (Several techniques exist for evaluating board performance; consultants and various tools are available for conducting a self-assessment.)

- Does an executive committee exist and is it being well used on behalf of the full board and the organization?

- What is the "profile" of the board by age, gender, race, education, profession, and giving and getting level? Given the current mission and the times, what is the desirable profile?

- Do certain members need to resign in order to open up slots or to remove deadwood?

- Given the desired profile of board membership, does a list of appropriate candidates exist and what is the plan for their recruitment?

The issue of conflict of interest by board members arises more often than it should, particularly with the boards of smaller or newer nonprofits, and is therefore worth further discussion. The most common conflict occurs when a board member stands to gain financially, as when the organization does business with a firm in which the board member has an interest. The principle is clear enough: board members are chartered to promote the interest of the organization, even in favor of their own, and must avoid not only the fact but the appearance of a conflict between the two. Unfortunately, many boards do not have an explicit policy and never discuss the matter; in those cases, conflicts frequently do arise. The chief executive who is aware that such a conflict exists is in a difficult position—often the board member in question will believe or profess that he or she is doing the organization a great favor. This is a matter that trustees must resolve among themselves; the chief executive's job is on the line with board members and the executive cannot be expected to do so.

The interaction of all of these rules and suggestions presents a conundrum: trustees are to remain firmly on the side of policy and to leave administration to management; most boards are too large for effective decision making; the institution needs trustees to feel involved and important. With these complications, how do you gain their effective participation without inviting micro-management?

Trustees who come to feel that their membership involves little more than listening to management report on decisions already made are apt to grow bored and to move on, either in fact or in their heads. The first to do so will be those who are most committed to action and whose support you would least like to lose. To solve this conundrum requires hard work, creativity, and close cooperation between the chief executive and the board leadership, especially the chair. The matter should be discussed openly with the committee on trusteeship and their suggestions sought on how to make the board operate so as to provide greater satisfaction to its members. Make all trustees understand that although major policy decisions occur infrequently, other important work goes on continually. A senior member of one board estimated that over his service of more than two decades, the board had made an average of only one or two major policy decisions annually. Obviously, the rest of the time the board was doing something else. Most new board members need to learn this lesson.

To help new board members get off to a good start and to get them thinking about your agenda, hold an orientation session at least once a year. When the date is selected, invite any trustee who is interested to attend; some more senior members may appreciate a refresher. The orientation should begin with a presentation by you followed by remarks by senior staff. If appropriate, the orientation can include a tour of the facility. This session provides a good way for you to have new trustees become part of your team and for you to begin to provide the board leadership for which this chapter calls.

Staying in touch with board members other than the chair without inviting micromanagement is difficult, especially at organizations with large boards, which can number forty, fifty, and more. Some executives invent reasons for contacting individual trustees, pretending to consult them on issues where their advice is not really wanted or needed. Most trustees will see through this at once and lose respect for the chief executive. Ask for advice only when you need it; when the advice makes sense, follow it.

A technique that many chief executives use effectively is to issue a monthly letter to the board, reporting recent developments and highlighting their own activities. This provides a useful forum for getting across important news and preparing the board for the next meeting.

A wise chief executive will spend some alone with each member of the board once a year and, in the case of the more influential trustees, more than once a year. When trustees view you as a near stranger, their reason for serving and your job security have diminished.

12

. . . .

Leaving Gracefully

Leaders should lead as far as they can and then vanish. Their ashes should not choke the fire they have lit.

H. G. Wells

The search for a new chief executive is a critical milestone in an institution's history. At a large one, a year or more and hundreds of thousands of dollars are often consumed in the process. The search for a new executive cannot commence, however, until the current occupant is known to be leaving and the position is scheduled to become vacant. Opening the vacancy thus is a necessary precursor to filling it; one cannot happen without the other. Usually, however, for reasons explained farther along in this chapter, little thought is given and little care is taken in how and when the position of chief executive becomes vacated. All institutional attention is concentrated on filling the vacancy and almost none on how and when it is created.

How Long to Serve?

The tenure of a typical chief executive is marked by a cycle. The new appointee arrives either already filled with ideas for change or soon develops them. An initial year or two of transition and team building are followed by several for testing and implementation. If the status-quoers can be overcome, change and progress occur. After a while, however, with rare exceptions, the supply of fresh ideas begins to run dry. Those that could be transplanted into the institution have been; others that would not take root have had to be discarded and can seldom be planted again. Although steps can and should be taken to replenish the chief executive's supply of new ideas, the process is unidirectional, subject to a kind of entropy. It is a rare chief executive who after eight to ten years continues to have new ideas that have yet to be tried and that have a good chance of being implemented.

In time, some members of the senior team—even those once recruited by the chief executive—will have grown tired and need replacement. After years of working closely with them and of evaluating them positively, however, it may be difficult for the chief executive to let them go, especially for staff members who were hired by the executive. Policies also wear out and need to be supplanted by new ones. But again, the chief executive who has approved each policy, often with fanfare and pride, finds them hard to jettison.

The chief executive who wishes to continue to inspire cannot become overly familiar or intimate. As time passes, though, the executive inevitably becomes better known, and the opportunity for inspirational leadership gradually wanes. The smaller the institution and the more directly involved the chief executive is in its affairs, the more rapidly this occurs. No exact timetable can be given, but experience would indicate that it is a rare individual who remains inspirational after eight to ten years in office.

All of us have seen chief executives who, while outwardly professing their enjoyment in the position, have aged before our eyes. Some individuals can handle a high level of stress, but others cannot or should not. For them, at some point, for the sake of health and family, enough is enough. Again, this point will vary with the individual and the institution, but even with a sound program of stress management, a chief executive will have accumulated much stress and frustration after eight to ten years at that institution. After FDR, who died in office, Congress passed the Twenty-second Amendment limiting presidents of the United States to two terms or eight years. That seems about right.

For all of these reasons, after the passage of a number of years that varies from case to case but which would generally fall within the range of eight to ten, progress has evolved about as far as one chief executive can take it. For the good of the institution, more change is required, but the current chief executive is no longer able to be an agent of change and the only good reason for serving has passed. It is time for a new leader to be found, one who can start the cycle of renewal and progress again, building on the foundation that the present chief executive has established.

Every rule has its exceptions. Two of the most successful and effective leaders in America are Frank Rhodes, president of Cornell for eighteen years, and Derek Bok, who served as president of Harvard for twenty. But these men are the giants on whose shoulders the rest of us would be fortunate to stand. Their special gifts of leadership allow them to be the exception. Unfortunately, there are many more examples of chief executives who stayed well beyond their time. The difficulty is that although most recognize that in the career cycle of a typical chief executive a period of optimum effectiveness is followed by decline, the barriers to departure are high.

Prolonging: The Institution's Stake

By the time eight to ten years have passed, the skillful chief executive will have assembled the right kind of board and its members will probably be satisfied with the executive. New appointees will have been hand picked; doubters will have been won over or dropped. Many will owe their presence on the board to the chief executive; a few may be friends; some will be disengaged and uninterested; the chief executive controls most of the information that the board receives and it appears to be largely favorable. Such a group is not apt to ask whether it is time to begin to look for a new chief executive.

Nevertheless, a few trustees, those who know that eight to ten years is long enough, will have begun to talk among themselves about succession. They may not find much support, and even those who agree will say that although things could be better, they are not so bad that a few more years cannot be borne. Perhaps during that time, the chief executive will get another job or, if not, can be counseled to improve or shored up with a strong number two (Fisher, 1991). A chief executive who reaches the eight- to ten-year period and is fifty-five to sixty years old has "only a few years to go"; it will be argued that the humane thing to do is to wait until the executive reaches age sixty-five. Thus, matters have to be in a sorry state before a board will ask a chief executive with eight to ten years of service to resign. Often the board asks not, "What could an optimally effective chief executive accomplish?" but rather, "Is our friend and colleague, the current executive, performing so poorly that replacement is mandatory?" That is the wrong question.

Here is an example in which board leadership lost effective control of the process by which the chief executive was appointed:

The controversial director of an art museum suddenly resigned. The board chose to appoint the deputy director for a five-year term, after which it was understood by board leaders that a full search would take place. The new director, however, though not particularly effective at the job, was able to become sufficiently popular with the board rank and file that the leaders thought they should reappoint him for a second term, producing in the end a decade of barely adequate leadership.

If this is how matters appear to the institution and to the board, how do they seem to the chief executive? Here too the weight is heavily on the side of staying longer.

Prolonging: The Chief Executive's Stake

The chief executive is enjoying career-high compensation and perquisites, neither likely to be matched in any position that might follow. The ego is continually salved as many tell you what a great job you are still doing. By this time, the chief executive and perhaps spouse have put down roots in the community. Friends, family, and church are here, not somewhere else. Moving is always an unhappy prospect and it grows worse with age. If you can handle the stress or make yourself believe that you are handling it, why leave if you do not have to?

But as Fisher (1991) wisely points out, deep down, each chief executive knows, in spite of the praise and the hopes expressed that the chief executive will be "president for life," when it is time to go. Even when a chief executive admits to this level of self-knowledge and is willing in principle to depart, doing so is difficult for many reasons.

You may not be able to look openly for another position without compromising the one you have. Trustees, who of course move frequently in their jobs, often expect that a nonprofit chief executive will be like a minister, "called" to the position to depart only when carried out on a stretcher (which has happened). A chief executive who would seek to leave is apt to be viewed as uncommitted, even disloyal. More than one chief executive has lost the position in exactly this way.

In addition, at this point in your career, you will have developed a good deal of pride in yourself and your work. To enter the job market, however, you must subject yourself to a possibly ignominious search process, at the end of which you may be rejected. This opens up the worst of all possible worlds: those at your home institution will learn that you are trying to leave but that apparently no other institution will have you. This is a risk that not many are willing to take. Here is a case where it proved fatal to a chief executive's career:

The director of a theater was recruited to head another in a nearby city. The theater that sought his candidacy received public monies, requiring that its search be conducted "in the sunshine." An article about the search and final candidates appeared in the newspaper of that city and was picked up by the candidate's hometown paper, which wrote an editorial saying that the director had done a poor job and ought to leave. This not only helped to deny the director the position he sought, it crystallized negative opinion about him at his home institution and within a year he was forced out.

There may be other problems related to job hunting. It is often difficult for chief executives to return to a staff or faculty position at the same institution because credentials have grown out of date; often a new period of training would be required and that is usually not feasible. Furthermore, a chief executive with eight to ten years of service is typically over fifty. In the second half of that decade of life, one's appeal and one's self-confidence may not be what they were. For your sake, and that of any family, you simply cannot take the risks that you might have taken ten years earlier.

For many chief executives, the question of when to leave is undoubtedly the most difficult of an entire career. Leave too early and you may damage yourself and your family and leave the job only half completed. Leave too late and the fine record of your early years may be besmirched; securing another position may be out of the question. Either way, the risk to family, to reputation, and to service is high.

Here is a rare example of a chief executive who knew herself and acted:

The new chief executive of a women's advocacy organization, who had served for years at another until she had begun to feel burned out there, arrived at her new post to great acclaim and with high hopes. Within eighteen months, however, as the job became more familiar, she noticed that she no longer became excited about new program options and was quickly frustrated as she found herself dealing with the same issues that she had handled for years in her previous post. Finally, counseling helped her to realize that she had not merely grown tired of her previous organization—she had burned out in this type of organization. She had the courage to begin a quiet search for a position in a different kind and was able to leave before her frustration and burnout became obvious to others.

Gilmore (1988) offers a useful way to think about the decision to leave by drawing an analogy with the need to let go of one's children. Just as the mother bird eventually must eject the fledgling from the nest, so every parent knows that at some time, for the good of the child, they must separate. Often the decision is painful for both; some relationships never fully recover. But the truly loving parent lets go. In the same way, whether you truly love the institution that you have been serving or whether your concern is more professional, in the nature of giving it your best, you must attempt to steel yourself and leave when the time comes. Good advice, I believe, but with so much at stake, it is enormously hard to put into practice. Is it advice that is simply so difficult to follow that leaders cannot be expected to do so? If that is the case, the nonprofit sector has a deep problem on a national scale.

A National Problem and a National Solution

Many institutional and individual motives, each understandable, combine to cause nonprofit chief executives to remain another year, and another. Those skillful (and lucky) enough to last for eight years can find them stretching to ten, to twelve, to fourteen, and by that time it really may be too late to do anything but wait it out. Although this is a larger issue than can be addressed by one institution and one chief executive, institutions can take steps to ease the difficulty. Search consultants and the more astute trustees are fully aware of the problem and should address it at the time a new chief executive is being hired. Below are three suggestions aimed at maximizing the effectiveness of the chief executive while in office and three that will make departure easier:

1. In order to provide some security, the chief executive should have a contract with a fixed term, say, three, four, or five years.

2. The chief executive should take a long vacation annually, most of it in a block and out of town if not out of the country, the farther away the better.

3. Depending on institutional size, after a certain period of service, the chief executive might receive a paid sabbatical leave for a specified number of months for the purpose of professional retooling and battery recharging.

4. The board chair and the chief executive should develop the kind of relationship that permits them to discuss the desirable length of the chief executive's tenure at least in general terms. The chair should understand that it is good for both the institution and the chief executive for the term not to extend indefinitely through inaction.

5. Sometime after six or seven years of service, without losing the confidence of the board chair, the chief executive should be able to establish contact with search consultants and enter a confidential search or two. Depending on how the chair views the chief executive, such exploration can be permitted or encouraged. The key is the openness of the relationship with the chair.

6. The wise chief executive will be fully aware of the inevitability of the cycle and will take action. Charles Glassick recommends that the executive treat the matter as a serious, almost scholarly, project (conveyed in a personal communication, 1993). Perform a rigorous evaluation of your effectiveness and of your enjoyment of your current position. Think hard about

the skills that you have developed that could be used in other types of organizations. Talk privately with colleagues and search consultants. As David Ellis suggests, the chief executive who has served for eight to ten years and who has a sabbatical can use that time for a careful search and as a stepping-stone to the next position (personal communication, 1993).

Nevertheless, even with this kind of activity, the dilemma really does transcend the ability of an individual institution or its chief executive to solve on their own. Rather the problem of chief executive succession affects the entire nonprofit sector and the entire sector ought to find a way to address it. One step that could be taken is for the major nonprofit professional associations, such as the American Council on Education, the American Association of Museums, the Association of Governing Boards, the Association of American Colleges, and others, to pool their resources and jointly establish a data bank of available positions that might be of interest to senior nonprofit chief executives. The data bank would list all the vacancies for the position of nonprofit chief executive, as well as for other senior positions below that level. Certain senior faculty positions might be listed as well (how much better for an academic ex-president to join the faculty of some other institution!). An office, well staffed and led by an experienced search consultant, could be established in Washington to manage this operation.

Locating the Acting Chief Executive

A chief executive leaving a nonprofit institution to retire can give a year's notice, allowing a careful search to be conducted. In other instances, however, when the executive is recruited away to another position or leaves under duress, the interval between announcement and departure is shorter, requiring the appointment of an acting chief executive. Usually the institution has no choice but to do so from within its own ranks, a procedure that has several disadvantages.

One is that the individual tapped to be acting chief executive must be replaced also from within and so on down the line, creating a set of dislocations to the organizational structure. Another is that although there are dramatic exceptions, generally the acting chief executive will lack some of the qualifications (and perhaps some of the motivation) necessary for success as a chief executive—otherwise why has not the individual already been tapped for such a position? And no matter how qualified, the acting chief executive will experience all the difficulties associated with newness to the position.

A third disadvantage is that if the acting chief executive would be a strong candidate for the permanent position, serving in an acting capacity may not help: one has all the responsibility of the position but even less of the authority and therefore cannot accomplish as much. As Gilmore (1988) notes, trustees often think that appointment to the acting role will allow an internal candidate to be tested, but it seldom works out that way. The seemingly tentative nature of the appointment may imply an ambivalence on the part of the board, leaving subordinates uncertain as to the acting chief executive's authority. For these and several other reasons, internal candidates often see their chances diminish steadily throughout a tenure as acting chief executive. If you are offered such a position, think it over carefully. You might be better off to decline and await discovery during the search; the search committee might be better off not to tip its hand too early in favor of the internal candidate.

Given the disadvantages of an acting appointment from inside, many institutions would be well served were there a cadre of available, experienced, and trained persons from outside who could step in for a few months up to perhaps as much as a year as acting chief executive. This happens now and again today, but depends more on coincidence than planning. These outsiders would bring many of the advantages discussed in Chapter Two (I repeat Gardner's quote in that chapter): "disinterested criticism, astringent appraisal, the rude question [and] judgments untainted by the loyalty and camaraderie of insiders, undistorted by the comfortable assumptions held within the walls" (1990, p. 130). They would also have the further benefit of emphatically not being a candidate for the position, tending to free their hands for tough but necessary decisions and clearing the way for the new, permanent chief executive.

A solution of this type would be particularly welcome at smaller institutions, where the possible choices for acting chief executive are limited, if they exist at all. Indeed, some religious organizations, facing the difficulty of finding a successor to serve as pastor of a small church that simply has no one else to appoint, have established training programs for former pastors so that they can serve in an acting capacity, giving time for a judicious selection of the next pastor and sustaining the congregation in the meantime.

Perhaps other nonprofit associations would be well advised to follow their example by establishing programs to train experienced chief executives, many of whom would need very little additional preparation, who could then step in as acting chief executive during a search. The opportunity to serve in an acting capacity might provide an appealing transition for some current chief executives, who know they ought to leave but have no where to go.

Suppose, for example, that a major professional association used its good offices to establish a data base of recently retired but still vigorous former chief executives who would be interested in interim appointments under the right conditions. The association could then conduct a one-month training program for these individuals in which they learned of the special problems facing an interim chief executive and brushed up on new developments. When a member institution needed an interim chief executive, the association could supply a list of several who could be interviewed confidentially. If none worked out, the institution could still turn to its internal choice, having lost only a small amount of time.

Epilogue

In many for-profit organizations, the chief executive is removed from the customer by layers of bureaucracy and distance. One of the great advantages of leadership in the nonprofit sector—one among many, in my opinion—is that the chief executive can easily be (and often is by necessity) in direct and daily contact with the people the organization serves. The museum director cannot help meeting with visitors, the library director with patrons, the social service agency director with clients, the academic president with students, and so forth. Few professions offer such immediate response and, when things go well, such immediate psychic reward for a job well done.

The person who leads a nonprofit organization has the golden opportunity to serve institutions that educate, heal, uplift, assist, explain, enlighten, interpret, support, beautify . . . In return, non-profit leaders must be willing to put up with a slower pace of change and less remuneration. Most of us who work in the sector believe that the bargain is a good one. The privilege of leading such institutions, however, demands from us the highest level of professional conduct. Indeed, service to such organizations must be placed far above self. Therefore, the decision to accept such a position should not be made casually, merely because it appears to be the next obvious step on a career ladder, or to gain pay, power, or prestige. It should be as carefully thought through as any major life decision, comparable, for example, to proposing or accepting marriage.

Once in a leadership position, while "fighting fair," the chief executive should do everything possible to bring about the maximum amount of positive change that the organization can sustain. Leadership must be pursued aggressively, with everything you have.

Finally, I offer these five key elements of effective nonprofit leadership, distilled from the many in this book:

1. Above all, maintain your integrity.

2. Be yourself.

3. Continually gauge your effectiveness, and when you find yourself coming up short, ask why and take action to correct the problem.

4. Improve and maintain your stamina and fitness.

5. When you know that you can no longer be an agent of change, resign and do something else.

To again quote JFK (who led a very large nonprofit organization):

> All this will not be finished in the first one hundred days. Nor will it be finished in the first one thousand days, nor in the life of this administration, nor even perhaps in our lifetime on this planet. But let us begin.

Resource A

· ·

Questions Asked at Job Interviews

Questions conceived by search committees naturally bear a certain similarity. A candidate can prepare by giving thought to appropriate answers to those listed below. In addition, candidates are apt to be asked for a brief biographical statement.

- What do you hope to be doing in ten years?

- What interests you about this position?

- What are your strengths and weaknesses?

- How do you deal with conflict?

- What does a chief executive do ideally?

- What has been your biggest success?

- What has been your most difficult administrative task?

- Describe your physical and mental health. (One candidate began to answer this question by noting that he had run five miles that very morning. A wag on the search committee responded, "Now please tell us about your physical health.")

- Have you ever fired anyone? Why, and how did you go about it?

· · · · ·

- What are your hobbies? (How do you relax?)

- What do you expect would be the greatest problem facing you in this position?

- How do you view the importance of diversity at our organization?

- What are you most proud of in your career?

- What made you choose your career?

- Who has been the most influential person in your life?

- What section of the newspaper do you read first?

- What are you reading these days?

- Tell us about your family (a question that probably should not be asked but may be).

- Do you like to entertain?

Resource B

· ·

Negotiating Terms and Conditions
of the Initial Employment Contract

As noted in Chapter Two, at the time you receive an offer to be a chief executive, you have the most leverage you will ever have with that organization and possibly ever again in your career. Use the opportunity to strike an agreement that is fair to you, to the institution, and to the profession.[*]

If either party feels that it has been exploited, the relationship may be brief. Ideally, when the negotiation is over, the new chief executive will feel appreciated and fairly rewarded and the institution will know that its chief executive is being well compensated. Then both can expect hard work and an excellent performance; fairness of compensation is no longer an issue to get in the way.

Below I describe a set of terms, some of which a nonprofit chief executive must have in his or her contract, some of which are optional. A few chief executives from larger institutions will have all and perhaps others that have been specially tailored. For the smaller institutions, many of these benefits and perquisites will not apply.

The new chief executive and the board need to be aware that, prompted by the example of a few bad apples, the compensation of nonprofit chief executives is coming under rising scrutiny. Further-

---

[*]Fisher (1991) has a more extensive coverage of this subject, with examples of contracts and so on.

more, government regulations increasingly limit the arrangements a nonprofit can make with its chief executive.

Financial Terms

The salary and benefit package should reflect the size and budget of the institution and the salaries of chief executives of similar ones. The salary should be independent of the chief executive's experience and age in the sense that a youngish chief executive should not be penalized—the job should pay what it pays.

The chief executive should have the same pension plan as other employees. If there is none, a generous program with an institutional contribution should be tailored. Some institutions have a waiting period before an employee can go onto the pension program; the chief executive should receive compensating salary until eligibility begins.

Although it is increasingly difficult, it may be desirable and possible that some compensation be deferred. The organization's lawyer will need to draw up any such arrangement.

The chief executive will receive the institution's medical and disability insurance package but may need special consideration in order to have adequate coverage.

Some chief executives, especially academic ones, are expected to live in a home owned by the institution. There is another side to the matter, however, that needs to be considered: the deduction on mortgage interest payments is almost the only tax shelter left to the average person. It should not be given up without careful study. Real estate historically has been a better investment than even the stock market. This has been less true in certain sections of the country over the last decade or so, but carefully chosen real estate should be a good bet over the long run. Someday the chief executive will have to leave the institutional home and buy another. Unless the executive has been frugal and disciplined, this may turn out to be a difficult transaction to fund. Finally, owning and living in one's own home may add to peace of mind. Unless it is essential that the chief executive live in the home supplied, ask whether the institution would instead provide you with a housing allowance adequate for you to buy your own, one suitable for institutional entertaining. The "President's Home" could still be used for entertaining or it could be sold. But before making a decision, obtain the advice of a financial and tax consultant. (Note: if you are to live in an institutional home, have any renovations done before you arrive; that way the expense will not reflect upon you personally.)

Some larger institutions provide the chief executive with a car and a budget for entertainment. Some pay the dues of private and airline clubs. But let your conscience be your guide as to which benefits to seek. If the institution can afford it, and if the expenditure will be made on its behalf rather than your own, then it is reasonable for the institution to pay for the perquisite.

Other Terms

The chief executive should receive a scheduled, automatic sabbatical leave. This schedule should continue for as long as the chief executive is in office.

The chief executive should receive an appointment with a definite and renewable term—three to five years.

The method by which the chief executive is to be evaluated and its timing should be agreed on (see Fisher [1991] for a more detailed discussion). This is an important but easily deferred matter. Most nonprofits do not think about how the chief executive should be evaluated until it is almost too late; then they conduct the evaluation by having a group, excluding the chief executive, that "sits around talking." After such a session, one chief executive subsequently was told, "You are too consultative; you have hired too many women; we do not approve that your spouse works." Beware, and negotiate your evaluation process as carefully as your salary—they will prove to be closely connected.

Although it is rare for an incoming chief executive to be actively concerned with termination, many should be, for the law of averages has not been repealed. Certainly, most of the business people on the institution's board will have a generous "golden parachute." Therefore, the initial contract should include a clause defining the arrangements to apply should the chief executive be terminated before the contract has expired. It should also cover dismissal for cause. Do not hesitate to discuss termination at the time of appointment; if you do not, it will immediately be too late to raise the matter. (A search consultant may be able to act as a useful intermediary).

Resource C

· ·

Your First Meeting with Senior Staff

As described in Chapter Three, as early as possible in the new position, ideally the morning of the first day, the new chief executive should meet with senior staff—the "direct reports"—to apprise them of the executive's expectations and preferred administrative style. Begin this meeting with a brief explanation of why you took the job and what you hope to accomplish with their help.

The following are the points that I have made in such meetings; they can be revised to suit the new chief executive's priorities and style:

This will be an open administration. There will be no secret documents, meetings, agreements, or understandings. Some matters such as individual salaries will of course be confidential, but the budget, the long-range plan, the names and business addresses of trustees, will be available to any employee (or student at academic institutions).

My staff should never surprise me. I will try never to surprise them. If in doubt, both will err on the side of disclosure.

I am responsible to the board. My staff is responsible to me. Therefore, my staff should never argue with me or compromise me in front of the board. I strongly discourage staff from having personal relationships with board members. I expect to be told in person or by memo whenever staff have a substantive conversation with a board member.

As chief executive, I seek good ideas. My staff should find time in their schedules to think about their jobs and the organization and to generate new ideas for improvement. I expect to be approached with such ideas continually; many will fail to bear fruit, in which case no penalty will be applied. In my administration, the people with ideas will thrive.

I am a delegator. I expect my staff to rise to the occasion.

I will meet weekly with my senior staff to share information. These are informational meetings rather than ones in which actions are to be approved through a democratic process. In areas where I have the responsibility and authority, after listening carefully and considering all the evidence, I will make the decision that I believe to be right.

We will avoid "groupthink." Many errors have been made when members of a group either are carried away by their own rhetoric or else no one sees the need or has the nerve to ask the tough questions. My senior staff should rotate the role of devil's advocate so as to avoid this phenomenon.

Decisions will be supported. Once a decision has been made through such a process, the day of the devil's advocate is over and each vice president must actively support the decision. Having had a chance to make the case, it is unprofessional then to step outside the advisory circle to criticize or to try to defeat the decision.

I too plan to generate ideas, suggestions, and requests. Some I will mention casually to one of you. In that case, you should consider the suggestion and if it seems to hold promise, follow it up. When a request is put in writing, however, I expect a reply in timely fashion. The response may be that after preliminary study the idea or suggestion appears not to be feasible, that the requested information is not available, or even that I was mistaken. *Some* reply, however, must be forthcoming. The chief executive cannot be put in a position of having to ask repeatedly for a response to a reasonable request.

I expect you to follow common sense regarding your schedules and your own stress management. Take all the vacation time you have coming; I will do the same. I want you to work more intelligently and reflectively rather than simply harder; workaholics will not be rewarded.

If you do not use a computer in your daily work, you must start to do so immediately. My first electronic mail message will soon be on its way!

I do not bring with me a new broom to sweep all from office. I respect your knowledge and service to the organization and I will give you ample time to prove yourselves. (Six months should be long enough for you to evaluate them.)

We will have fair and mutually acceptable methods of evaluation. I will work with each of you to develop such a method.

I expect you to grow and advance in your jobs and in your careers and I will help you. I assume that some of you will receive offers from other institutions and in time will move on. That is what happens in a healthy organization.

Resource D

Asking for Major Donations
A Scenario

Fisher Howe (1991, pp. 87–92) outlines an excellent, step-by-step approach to asking a prospect for a gift, from which the following is excerpted and adapted.

Preparation

Before finding yourself in the presence of a prospective donor, you will have satisfied these conditions:

- You have the right prospect.

- You have cultivated your prospect.

- You know the prospect's interests.

- You will see the prospect in person.

- You know the amount for which you will ask.

The "Birdies"

From the moment you walk in the door for your solicitation visit, like any salesperson, keep your eyes on four "birdies":

1. The purpose of the visit is to ask for money. Everything about the conversation should relate to that. Do not find yourself saying goodbye without having popped the question.

2. Talk opportunities, not needs. Donors give where they think they will make a difference. They are not interested in your institution's needs—they want to know what their gift will permit you to do.

3. Stay sensitive to what your prospect is thinking while you are talking. Do not be mesmerized by the sound of your own voice and your well-rehearsed presentation.

4. Begin, be brief, be off. Do not race, but do not linger—get on with your purpose and get out.

The Scenario Itself

No two solicitations are the same, but here is a reasonable scenario:

1. Open with pleasantries. However, discuss something related to the prospect rather than the weather.

2. Get to the subject. Begin with "thanks for seeing me" and ask if you can bring the prospect up-to-date about your institution.

3. Get to the asking. Always put your request in terms of an opportunity and suggest a specific donation. Mention the figure you have in mind early and only once.

4. Be ready for any of a number of negative responses. A flat refusal leaves little room; exit as quickly and politely as you can. Some initial negatives are not necessarily refusals, for example, "You've got me in the wrong league." Leave the request on the table.

5. Leave on a positive note. If you have been turned down, keep the solicitation open—rarely do you get a commitment on the spot.

6. In all cases, follow up promptly with a note, a tactful reminder that the solicitation is still open.

Resource E

· ·

Learning to Use the Computer

Today every professional and certainly every chief executive needs to have some familiarity with the device that is transforming the world: the personal computer. Even if your career began before its advent, it is not too late to begin to learn. By following the program that I outline below and spending an average of an hour per day and four on weekends, within a month you will have learned to use a computer well enough to improve your productivity. Following the same schedule, and by using the computer more and more at work, within a few months the way you work will have been changed forever; you will be back in the mainstream. The time you invest will be amply repaid in gains in productivity and quality.

Get started by buying a mid- to upper-level laptop computer (make sure that it has a full-sized keyboard) that you can use both at home and at work. This machine should have a 200 megabyte hard disk, 12 megabytes of RAM, and a bundle of software such as Microsoft Office. The display should be of high quality but need not provide color. The machine should be compatible with the desktop computer that you will eventually use at work. It is not necessary to purchase a printer at this stage, but make sure that you have a way to print at your office. Get yourself one of the instruction books for novices and a set of training tapes for your word processing software. You might enroll in a local course in computing for beginners or have a tutor come to your office.

When using a computer for the first time, you are sure at least once to be stymied by something that should be obvious but is not. The classic example is an inability to locate the switch that turns the machine on! When such a problem arises, you need to find a person to whom you can turn for help without embarrassment. Let someone who is more expert—your spouse, a friend, a trusted staff associate—in on your self-improvement plan so that they can give help when you need it.

Now you are ready to begin—except for a little secret that it is time we got out in the open: you never learned to touch-type! You must now take the time to learn, otherwise the benefits of the computer will be largely denied to you. Furthermore, it is much easier to learn to type nowadays than it was in the high school course that you avoided or have largely forgotten. Along with the equipment above, buy yourself a copy of a sophisticated typing instruction software program. To the program of self-instruction described below, add a half hour a day for learning to touch-type. Within two weeks, you will be typing twenty words per minute, as fast as you can write legibly by hand. Stick with it another two, and you will be up to thirty to thirty-five wpm, fast enough to make typing your preferred mode of writing. Then, as you begin to use the computer more and more, your typing speed will rise to its natural level.

Your program of self-instruction should then follow this sequence:

1. Read the *Getting Started* or similarly-titled booklet that comes with your computer (the system and other software should have been installed by the seller). If a tutorial file is available, locate it and follow instructions. (On a new Macintosh, for example, it is called "Macintosh Basics.") You will learn the minimal functions of the machine: how to use the mouse and windows, to find files, to save your work. In less than an hour or two, you will be ready to move on.

2. Read a chapter or two each night in the instruction book, but stop when you overload.

3. Your word processing software will include a tutorial file; open it and follow instructions. It will also provide you with a manual with a title like *Getting Started*. Alternate between trying the tutorial and reading this manual; do not attempt to read the complete reference manual—they have evolved into enormous tomes.

4. Once you feel that you understand how to use the basic functions of the computer and have followed the introduction to your software, start to use the instructional tapes.

5. Continue to cycle between reading, using the instructional tapes, and practicing on documents of your own.

6. As you begin to feel more comfortable with the word processor with which you began, order a set of training tapes for your spreadsheet and repeat the process.

By the end of the first month or six weeks, you will be using your word processor for routine writing, composing on the keyboard, and sending drafts over the network to your assistant for editing, formatting, and printing. You will understand how a spreadsheet works and can then decide whether that is enough for your purposes or whether you want to become more expert.

References

Acton, Lord. *Letter to Bishop Mandell Creighton*, Apr. 5, 1887. In J. Kaplan (ed.), *Bartlett's Familiar Quotations*. (16th ed.) Boston: Little, Brown, 1992.

Bass, B. *Leadership and Performance Beyond Expectations*. New York: Free Press, 1985.

Bass, B. *Bass & Stodgill's Handbook of Leadership: Theory, Research, and Managerial Applications*. (2nd ed.) New York: Free Press, 1990.

Bell, D. *Power, Influence, and Authority: An Essay in Political Linguistics*. New York: Oxford University Press, 1975.

Bennis, W. *The Leaning Ivory Tower*. San Francisco: Jossey-Bass, 1973.

Browning, R. "Andrea del Sarto." In M. Abrams (ed.), *Norton Anthology of English Literature*, Vol. 2. New York: W.W. Norton, 1962.

Bryson, J. M. *Strategic Planning for Public and Nonprofit Organizations*. San Francisco: Jossey-Bass, 1988.

Burns, J. M. *Leadership*. New York: HarperCollins, 1978.

Burns, R. "To a Mouse." In M. Abrams (ed.), *Norton Anthology of English Literature*, Vol. 2. New York: W.W. Norton, 1962.

Chaffee, E. E., and Sherr, L. A. "Total Quality Management." In T. D. Connors (ed.), *The Nonprofit Management Handbook: Operating Policies and Procedures* (pp. 3–22). New York: Wiley, 1993.

Cohen, M. D., and March, J. G. *Leadership and Ambiguity*. (2nd ed.) Boston: Harvard Business School Press, 1986.

Connors, T. D. (ed.). *The Nonprofit Management Handbook: Operating Policies and Procedures* (pp. 53–70). New York: Wiley, 1993.

Coolidge, C. *Autobiography of Calvin Coolidge*. New York: Cosmopolitan Book, 1929.

Drucker, P. F. *Managing for the Future.* New York: Viking Penguin, 1986.

Drucker, P. F. *The New Realities.* New York: HarperCollins, 1989.

Drucker, P. F. "What Business Can Learn from Nonprofits." *Harvard Business Review,* Jul.–Aug. 1989, 88–93.

Drucker, P. F. *Managing the Non-profit Organization: Principles and Practices.* New York: HarperCollins, 1990.

Fisher, J. L. *Power of the Presidency.* New York: Macmillan, 1984.

Fisher, J. L. *The Board and the President.* New York: Macmillan, 1991.

Fisher, J. L., and Quehl, G. (eds.). *The President and Fund-raising.* New York: Macmillan, 1989.

French, J.R.P., and Raven, B. (eds.). *The Bases of Social Power.* Ann Arbor: University of Michigan, Institute for Social Research, 1959.

Galbraith, J. K. *The Anatomy of Power.* Boston: Houghton Mifflin, 1983.

Gardner, J. *On Leadership.* New York: Free Press, 1990.

Gardner, J., and Reese, F. *Quotations of Wit and Wisdom.* New York: W.W. Norton, 1975.

Gaul, G., and Borowski, N. "Nonprofits: America's Growth Industry." *Philadelphia Inquirer,* April 18, 1993, p. 1.

Gilmore, T. N. *Making a Leadership Change.* San Francisco: Jossey-Bass, 1988.

Goethe, J. W. von. *Wilhelm Meister's Apprenticeship.* London: Dent, 1912.

Greenfield, J. M. *Fund-raising: Evaluating and Managing the Fund Development Process.* New York: Wiley, 1991.

Greenfield, J. M. "Fund-Raising Assessment." In T. D. Connors (ed.), *The Nonprofit Management Handbook: Operating Policies and Procedures* (pp. 647–694). New York: Wiley, 1993.

Hamilton, N. *JFK: Reckless Youth.* New York: Random House, 1992.

Herman, R. D., and Heimovics, R. D. *Executive Leadership in Nonprofit Organizations: New Strategies for Shaping Executive-Board Dynamics.* San Francisco: Jossey-Bass, 1991.

Homer. *The Odyssey.* In *Britannica Great Books,* Vol. 4. Chicago, London, Toronto: Encyclopedia Britannica, Inc., 1952.

Howe, F. *The Board Member's Guide to Fund Raising.* San Francisco: Jossey-Bass, 1991.

Humes, J. C. *Standing Ovation: How to Be an Effective Speaker and Communicator.* New York: HarperCollins, 1988.

Jenks, J. M., and Kelly, J. M. *Don't Do. Delegate!* New York: Ballantine, 1985.

Kissinger, H. *Years of Upheaval.* Boston: Little, Brown, 1982.

Knauft, E. B., Berger, R. A., and Gray, S. T. *Profiles of Excellence: Achieving Suc-*

cess in the Nonprofit Sector. San Francisco: INDEPENDENT SECTOR and Jossey-Bass, 1991.

Lao-Tzu. *The Way of Life*. (W. Bynner, trans.) New York: Putnam, 1944.

Lynch, R. *Lead!* San Francisco: Jossey-Bass, 1993.

Machiavelli, N. *The Prince*. New York: Knopf, 1992.

Mackay, A. *The Harvest of a Quiet Eye*. New York: Putnam, 1944.

McNamara, P. (ed.). *Testing the Operation and Effectiveness of a Nearly Complete Prototype Exhibit*. Washington, D.C.: Association of Science and Technology Centers, 1991.

Nash, O. "Quotable Quotes," *Reader's Digest*, 106(98), Feb. 1975.

O'Connell, B. *The Board Member's Book*. (2nd ed.) New York: The Foundation Center, 1993.

Parkinson, C. *Parkinson's Law*. London: John Murray, 1957.

Peter F. Drucker Foundation for Nonprofit Management. *The Drucker Foundation Self-Assessment Tool for Nonprofit Organizations*. San Francisco: Jossey-Bass, 1993. Ten workbooks and one instruction manual.

Pocock, J. W. *Fund-Raising Leadership: A Guide for College and University Boards*. Washington, D.C.: Association of Governing Boards of Universities and Colleges, 1989.

Public Management Institute. *The Effective Nonprofit Executive Handbook*. 1980.

Rossi, P., and Freeman, H. E. *Evaluation—A Systematic Approach*. (5th ed.) Newbury Park, Calif.: Sage, 1993.

Senge, P. *Fifth Discipline: The Art and Practice of the Learning Organization*. New York: Doubleday, 1990.

Shakespeare, W. *The Complete Works*. London: Collins, 1951.

Sorensen, T. *Kennedy*. New York: HarperCollins, 1965.

Stevens, F., Lawrenz, F., and Sharp, L. *User-Friendly Handbook for Project Evaluation*. Washington, D.C.: National Science Foundation, 1994.

Te'eni, D., and Speltz, N. "Management Information Systems in Cultural Institutions." In D. R. Young, R. M. Hollister, and V. A. Hodgkinson, and Associates, *Governing, Leading, and Managing Nonprofit Organizations*. San Francisco: Jossey-Bass., 1993.

Thoreau, H. *Walden*. New York: Penguin, 1960.

Truman, H. *Quote Magazine*, 49(12), Mar. 21, 1965, 2.

Twain, M. *The Lost Napoleon: Europe and Elsewhere*. New York: HarperCollins, 1923.

Twain, M. *Pudd'nhead Wilson*. New York: Penguin Books, Signet Classic, 1964.

Weber, M. *The Theory of Social and Economic Organization*. (M. Henderson and
     T. Parson, trans.) New York: Oxford University Press, 1947.

Wills, G. *Lincoln at Gettysburg*. New York: Simon & Schuster, 1992.

Worth, M. (ed.). *Fund-Raising: Principles and Practices*. Phoenix, Ariz.: Oryx,
     1993.

Young, D. "Nonprofit Management Education Comes of Age: A Progress
     Report." *Nonprofit World*, 8(6), Nov.–Dec. 1990, 17–19.

Index